Leslie Brooke
and Johnny Crow

Leslie Brooke
and Johnny Crow

by
Henry Brooke

FREDERICK WARNE

First Published in Great Britain
by Frederick Warne (Publishers) Ltd
London 1982

ISBN 0 7232 2878 7

Printed in Great Britain by
Butler & Tanner Ltd
Frome and London

Contents

I   A Stroke of Destiny

As far back into childhood as he could remember, Leslie Brooke wanted to be an artist when he was grown up. 'My brother and I were always drawing, like any other children,' he once wrote, 'and I went on drawing; there is my whole story.'

But it might have been otherwise. He could have been baulked of his ambition. Then as now, the profession of artist was a speculative one to plan to live on, not to be entered upon lightly unless one had genius. He might have had to yield to pressure to turn his natural gifts towards earning a less precarious livelihood in some more secure walk of life, had not a stroke of misfortune turned out to be a stroke of destiny. It was a happening for which countless children and their parents have cause to be grateful.

Birkenhead, where he was born on 24 September 1862 and where he spent the first twenty years of his life, was at that time a countrified town behind its shipbuilding waterfront on the Mersey. From the back door of their garden he and his brother Henry, two years his senior, could go straight out into the Wirral countryside to walk or to follow the beagles. Their father, Leonard Brooke, born in 1825, had grown up and gone to school and university in Dublin, and in 1856 he married Rhoda, daughter of Henry Leslie Prentice, of Caledon, Co. Tyrone. That was how they came to choose the names of Leonard Leslie for their second son. At home he was always Leslie, to distinguish him from his father, and he used to sign himself 'L. Leslie Brooke' all his life.

His father, who had been junior partner, in the course of time became sole head and owner of a small family business: Aspinall, Son and Brooke, rope and sail manufacturers. He commuted, as we should now say, daily across the Mersey to his office in Liverpool. In those days there was neither train tunnel nor road tunnel under the river, and all his life his son Leslie retained a nightmare recollection of once crossing the Mersey in dense fog and looking up suddenly to catch sight of the bow of an ocean liner towering above the deck of the little ferry boat.

They were Liverpool's mightiest years, the era of the saying, 'a Liverpool gentleman: a Manchester man'. One day the two boys, out with their father for a walk, noticed men with pegs and tapes and instruments working in the fields. Leonard Brooke told his sons that they were surveyors studying the possibility of a projected Ship Canal to link Manchester with the sea, which might ruin Liverpool by depriving her of the cotton trade. A hundred years later, Liverpool had lost the cotton trade and had lost the transatlantic liners; but she is still a city and a famous port.

Those were the nineteenth-century days when the great Mersey-side businesses, some of which became household words later on, were still in family hands. Cammell Laird, Birkenhead shipbuilders, were then John Laird and Son. Two letters from John Laird of those days to Leslie Brooke's father have survived, one asking permission to put his name forward for consideration as a Justice of the Peace, and one explaining that a vacancy had arisen for an Alderman on the Birkenhead Town Council and that it was the general wish that Mr Leonard Brooke should consent to be nominated.

Characteristically, he declined the second invitation, but accepted the first. Although he was a classical scholar and a widely read and cultured man, the shyness of his nature led him to shun the limelight. Honourable and meticulous in his business affairs, and prominent in many forms of voluntary service in his home town, he shrank from public speaking and controversy.

He dearly loved all his three children, Henry, Leslie and Rhoda, and on Sunday evenings when the two boys were small he used to play a game with them. Each in turn named an animal, and their father then had to think of something which that animal did or said or experienced 'in Johnny Crow's Garden'. The important rule was that it had to rhyme. Of course many animals and their doings were repeated from Sunday to Sunday. 'The Lion had a green and yellow tie on' was one of the favourites, and it was naturally and predictably followed by 'The Bear had nothing to wear'. Every now and then one boy or the other would introduce a new creature, and thereupon their obedient father would have to think of a new rhyme, which, if not very happy, would be forgotten, but if it was successful it would be added to the tradition. Children, when they are enjoying something, do not object to repetition; they revel in it.

Nobody now knows who Johnny Crow was, or how he got that name, or why or when or where he had a garden. Nobody sought to know. For two small boys in Birkenhead, Johnny Crow's Garden was an essential and unquestioned part of weekly life, a territory which their father populated for them with kindly animals behaving themselves enterprisingly and amusingly in rhyme. There was no continuity of story in those days. Each animal entered in as a test of their father's ingenuity. It was a verbal and unrecorded game, and there were no drawings at that stage, not even of Johnny Crow himself.

The game lapsed as the boys grew older. In due course they went to Birkenhead School, where both distinguished themselves academically, particularly in Latin and Greek. But Leslie made the most of his opportunities to illustrate his textbooks in the margin. Dr Pearse, the headmaster, taking Caesar's Gallic War with the top form,

Leslie Brooke as a schoolboy

9

noticed young Brooke drawing, and told him to bring up to him whatever it was. It turned out to be a dynamic sketch of Caesar throwing his legions across the river, in the manner of an athlete throwing a discus. He watched the stern face of the headmaster relax into the suspicion of a smile, swiftly suppressed; and the expected reprimand was softened to: 'Quite clever, boy—but get on with your work.'

In those youthful days the boys used to look forward to one holiday each year which was outstanding. Their uncle by marriage, Canon Armstrong, was the rector of Caledon, a village in Co. Tyrone near the border with Co. Monaghan, which fifty years later became the border between Northern Ireland and the Republic. He and his wife Isabella lived at The Glebe, and there was fishing in the lake nearby. Henry and Leslie were trusted to travel alone by the overnight boat from Liverpool, and their uncle met them at Kingstown and took them home to Caledon for two blissful weeks. No doubt their life-long enthusiasm for fishing, which Leslie had too little opportunity to gratify in later years, originated with these enchanted days at Caledon. These holidays also helped to familiarise them with Ireland and Irish ways of life and thought.

Leslie Brooke's diary for the year 1877, when he was fourteen to fifteen years old, has survived. He conscientiously kept it up right through the year. Not a day is blank. It is not a work of high imagination, but simply a straightforward boyish record of how each day was spent. Disappointingly it contains no drawings, and it might be the factual diary of any schoolboy distinguished only by the constant references to drawing and painting. Saturday 23 June 1877 is typical:

> 'School in morn. Half holiday. Drew in chalk and had painting lesson. Lawn tennis, chalk drawing and term book reading in evening.'

He enjoyed cricket too, and that winter he played football for the school 2nd XV. The diary conveys the impression of a full and happy life, at school and at home. There is no doubt about the happiness, for in later life he often testified to that, but perhaps it was a little too full. The evidence for this is that, when he had boys

10

of his own, he determined that they should go to boarding schools, and his reason, which he told them, was an interesting one. He thought that when he and his brother had been fifteen or sixteen or seventeen, their parents, to whom both boys were devoted, had taken for granted that they could live two lives in one: a school life of increasingly hard work and responsibility, and in the evenings a social life which meant taking their place as sons of the house and helping to entertain friends and relations who were invited to dinner. It enabled the boys to meet many older and interesting people and no doubt widened their outlook, and no lasting harm was done. But in later life they looked back on that as a time of strain when the constant necessity of adjustment between school life and home life made it hard for them to give unreservedly of their best to either.

In 1878 the elder brother Henry, who had been head of the school by then, went up to Exeter College, Oxford, where in due course he took a Second in Classical Mods and a Second in History Finals. The idea was that Leslie should follow him to Oxford two years later. But it did not work out that way.

In the early part of 1880 an aunt of theirs, Mrs Symes, invited Leslie, then seventeen and a half, to accompany her and her daughter for a three-month holiday travelling in Italy. He had never before been farther afield than Ireland, and this was a golden opportunity not to be missed. In a specially bound book with 'Italy—L.L.B.' in gilt lettering on the cover, probably given to him by his parents, he kept a meticulous diary of all he saw and did, and illustrated it with vignette sketches of people who caught his eye on the journey. A sketch book went with him everywhere, and frequently he seems to have done a quick pencil sketch in it, and then, if he thought it was good enough, he would copy it into the diary when he got back in the evening to the hotel where they were staying.

The scrappy writing of the 1877 diary, by a fourteen-year-old schoolboy in a hurry, has been replaced three years later by a controlled flowing script, neat and easy to read, that presages the beautiful handwriting in which all Leslie Brooke's grown-up letters were written. The Italy diary runs to some 20,000 words, and scarcely one is corrected or scratched out. True, he was almost

11

certainly writing the account for his parents to read when he returned home after the long holiday, but the combination of carefulness and freedom in his writing is an early pointer to the qualities of his illustrations in the picture books which were to make his name.

It quickly became obvious that whereas the intention of Mrs Symes and her daughter was to see the sights of Italy, Leslie Brooke's special purpose was to see the art. Starting from Turin, they stayed in Genoa, Spezia, Pisa, Naples, Sorrento and Rome, and wherever there were pictures in galleries he went not just to see them but to study them. Of every picture which impressed him he would record in his diary that same evening the subject and the painter and the feelings it aroused in him. The language of the diary is, to modern eyes and ears, a trifle self-conscious; but if his parents hoped that this visit to Italy would implant in him an appreciation of the Old Masters leading to a deep and understanding love, this hope was amply fulfilled. He never had a similar chance to revisit Italy, but at the age of seventeen each of the great Italian painters came alive for him, and his love for them never faded.

The language of the diary creates the picture of a serious-minded boy, determined to make the most of a wonderful holiday, vigorous, with wide interests, not afraid of committing his own judgments to paper even if sometimes they were naively expressed. It shows a knowledge of great art rare in a seventeen-year-old, the foundation for a discriminating taste in later life.

Those who know Leslie Brooke's children's books would hardly think of him as serious-minded. In the diary perhaps it was a veneer of serious-mindedness, designed to create an impression on those at home who had agreed to send him on this marvellous holiday. But even the supreme wonders of Italy could not suppress his sense of humour. One day a little boy offered to guide him from the place where the carriage-road ended to a monastery up on a hill which was his aim. The boy had such an attractive face that he gave him a few coins and made a sketch of him.

'There was another boy with him, who also wanted very much to have his portrait taken, so when I had done the first, I made him stand up, and pretended to make a sketch of him, all the while drawing a donkey's head, much to the delight of the good-looking

Sketches in diary of
Italian holiday, 1880

Notes at
the Roman Amphi-
theatre of the present
day

The English
jockey from a
Swedish point
of view.

The result
of civilisation.

one who looked over my shoulder all the time. I tore it out when I had finished it and gave it to the original, who seemed rather surprised at first at his appearance, but was afterwards much amused and seemed to take it rather as a compliment than otherwise.' (Diary for 12 March 1880, near Sorrento.) This was a foretaste of the Leslie Brooke of the children's books: always imaginative, always ready to add to the amusing side of life, never cruel, always leading a victim of ridicule towards the point of laughing at himself.

The diary of the Italian holiday stops abruptly. Leslie Brooke caught typhoid and was taken critically ill. After a time of great anxiety he recovered, and was able to return home to England completely fit again in all respects except one. His hearing was affected. Though he never became stone-deaf, from that time on to the end of his life his deafness gradually worsened, and was incurable.

It became immediately clear that a person partially deaf could not participate sufficiently in the work of a university which at that time taught almost entirely by lectures. The idea of Oxford must be given up, and he must plan and equip himself for a life where the handicap of deafness would matter little. His passion for drawing and painting furnished the direct and obvious answer. What had hitherto pointed away from his earning his daily bread as an artist now pointed directly towards it. There was no family opposition now to his committing himself to the life which inspired his ambition and gave him his delight. At the age of eighteen he entered the Birkenhead Art School.

II   On His Own

The Birkenhead Art School was excellent for his immediate needs, and he enjoyed it. But his heart was soon set on London as the city in which to continue his education, and at twenty he secured a place at the St John's Wood Art School, now defunct, but at that time situated in Elm Tree Road, with a high reputation and in a part of London where many artists had their studios and were close at hand to teach. He left home and took rooms at 66, St Mary's Terrace, near Maida Vale and within a mile of his place of work.

Only a few weeks later, he was recalled to Birkenhead by telegram. His father had suffered a tragic accident, from which it was doubtful if he ever fully recovered. He had been returning from work one evening on the top of a horse-drawn tram, and as he rose from his seat he was caught by a wire stretched too low across the street, and thrown down on the roadway. His injuries were severe, and though he survived the shock of them he was never the same again. Three years later, at the early age of sixty, he died.

The elder son Henry, who had just come down from Oxford and was starting to train himself to understudy his father in the family business, found responsibilities thrust upon him sooner than anyone had expected, and on his father's death, when he was only twenty-five, he had to take over the ownership and management of the business.

Leslie, now that his father was gravely ill, volunteered to give up London forthwith, and enter the business or do anything else which would help. But the others would not hear of his making this self-sacrifice, unless it turned out to be absolutely necessary, which it did not.

His mother, his brother Henry and his sixteen-year-old sister Rhoda lived on in Birkenhead, with Henry now the breadwinner. So Leslie, until he married, still had their house as his home base, and he travelled back there to see them whenever opportunity offered. But from 1882 onward he really became a Londoner.

In his studies his next ambition was to qualify for entrance to the Royal Academy Art Schools, and this he achieved in March, 1884, when he was twenty-one. He soon began exhibiting at small galleries; in 1885 he had three pictures in the North Kensington Fine Arts Exhibition. It was two years after this that he first had a picture, a watercolour of Bunbury Church in Cheshire, accepted by the Royal Academy for their summer exhibition at Burlington House. He crowned his student days at the Royal Academy Art Schools in 1888 by winning the First Armitage Prize, £30 and a bronze medal, for a life study, officially described as 'a design in monochrome for a figure picture'. He was modest about his Armitage Prize, but it was evidence for all to see that his hope of making a name for himself by his art was not a vacuous one.

London can be a lonely place for a young man who has come to work there but is not a Londoner born. Having this in mind, Leslie's father had written to some friends in London when Leslie first went up there in 1882, telling them about this son of his and how greatly he would appreciate any kindness they could show or any occasional hospitality they could offer him. Among the replies he received was one from an elderly man and wife living in a large house at Richmond, who gave Leslie a standing invitation to come to supper with them any Sunday evening he liked. They were charming people and the husband was something of a connoisseur of paintings, so Leslie went there from time to time and always enjoyed himself. Of course he looked at all the pictures, and particularly at one hanging on a dark wall under the stairs, which struck him as uncommonly like the work of Frans Hals. But if it really were by Frans Hals, he argued to himself, his host would certainly have recognised it as such, and hung it where it could be properly seen and appreciated. Not wanting to seem to pit his own youthful judgment against the lifelong experience of a much older man of acknowledged renown in the art world, he thought it wisest to say nothing.

Half a century later, a hitherto unknown Frans Hals turned up in a London auction-room. It fetched what was in those days a large sum. Because its history was a mystery, photographs of it appeared in the papers, and one of these caught Leslie Brooke's eye. He recognised it instantly as the picture on the dark wall under the stairs.

Another person to whom his father had written was a distant cousin, the Rev. Stopford Brooke, one of the great preachers of the day, art critic and writer, who lived at 1, Manchester Square in central London. Here too Leslie was made ever welcome, the more so as there were seven of Stopford Brooke's children in the house, the eldest twenty-four years of age, the youngest ten. Their mother, whom they had all worshipped, was dead, and their father's sister, 'Aunt Cecilia', had come to live with him to help in the upbringing of the younger ones. Physically and mentally Stopford Brooke was a formidable figure, but he was ready to talk on art with anyone who truly cared about it, and young Leslie Brooke fitted in with the ethos of this household more smoothly and happily than a business or professional man of his age, coming from outside, might have done.

From a sketchbook
of 1888

Meanwhile he was throwing himself unremittingly into his work at the Art Schools, and making new friends among his fellow students. Two at least of these friendships proved lifelong. This started with the three deciding to share rooms together—Clement Skilbeck ('Clem') and William Parkinson ('Togs') and Leslie Brooke. Thirty years later, happily married and fathers of families, all three had houses and studios within a stone's throw of one another in St John's Wood, still an artists' neighbourhood.

They were bound together by their quickness to sketch and by a common sense of humour. Generally started by Willie Parkinson, their stories about the successive landladies who provided them with board and lodging lost nothing in the telling. One of these excellent women had the habit of introducing them to the food she put before them for their suppers, somewhat like the experience of Alice in *Through the Looking Glass*. One day she placed before them a not particularly appetising dish with the words 'just a little bit of goat's lung'. Another evening, Willie averred, she introduced the first course as 'just a drain of foul soup'.

From a sketchbook

For exercise in these London days Leslie enjoyed fencing and dancing, as well as going for long walks. He was a better than average dancer, as his partners discovered, and this was principally because, as with so much else throughout his life, he set himself standards and kept up to them.

Leslie Brooke was twenty-six when he completed his course as an art student and turned to the full-time task of earning his living as a freelance artist. It was sink or swim, for since his father's death he could not rely on financial help from home, even had he wished to, which he did not. His enthusiasm for his chosen career never flagged. He managed to pick up commissions for book illustrations and book covers from a number of publishers, starting with Blackie and Cassell, and going on to Fisher Unwin and Dent. As a boy he had spent hours with pen and ink, copying Tenniel's drawings which he loved, and he slipped easily and naturally into pen and ink drawing for illustrations to books and stories. In 1889 Blackie asked him to illustrate *Thorndyke Manor* by Mary Rowsell, a novel for boys about Jacobite times. He did a set of telling black-and-white drawings for a new edition of Trollope's *Barchester Towers*. He succeeded Walter Crane in 1891 as the illustrator of Mrs Molesworth's annual children's story book published by Macmillan, and this made his work more widely known. The following year he also illustrated a collection of fairy stories, *Brownies and Roseleaves*, by Roma White.

He experimented, too, with portraits in oils. After his father's death he had attempted a posthumous portrait of him, which gave his mother much pleasure. A portrait of Stopford Brooke's brother, General Brooke—'Uncle Edward', one of the finest, simplest and handsomest of men—was hung in the 1889 Academy. But he was always more at home with pen, pencil, crayon and watercolour. Only one landscape of his in oils is known, and that hardly finished. He used to say that the best oil painting he ever did was a portrait of his mother, towards the end of her life. It mirrored her warmth, kindness and dignity in widowhood. Years later, unhappily, it suffered accidental damage too severe to remedy.

When Leslie Brooke was thirty, he met a Scotsman named J. M. Barrie, two years his senior, and better known in those days as an author than as a dramatist. *Peter Pan* had not yet appeared. He asked Barrie if he would sit to him, and Barrie, recognising that here was a young man with a swiftly responsive sense of humour, agreed. The portrait won its way into the Academy of 1896. Leslie Brooke never considered it to be one of his best, but the sittings led on to a pleasant friendship.

Predictably, these sittings were not easy to fix in advance, and thus they came to extend over a prolonged period. In the summer of 1893, before they had started, Barrie wrote from Kirriemuir: 'I hope to be in London in two or three months. Meanwhile the sun is painting me in various colours itself, and I shall watch the results with the view of telling you whether I like myself best in brown, white or red.'

Once the sittings began, they were enjoyed by artist and sitter alike. Barrie used to bring along to the studio his huge dog, the predecessor of Nana in *Peter Pan*. He would induce the dog to stretch its great length on the studio floor, just behind the painter's feet as he stood at the easel. Consequently when he stepped back, as painters do, to view the canvas from a greater distance, he would inevitably stumble over the recumbent dog. This became a well-worn joke; Barrie maintained that the dog was testifying to the superiority of the man of letters over the man of art.

III Marriage

A new life opened for Leslie Brooke when in December 1893 he became engaged to Sybil, youngest but one of Stopford Brooke's six handsome daughters. She was twenty-three; he was thirty-one, a trifle below medium height, with dark brown hair which turned silver grey in later years, but never white. Both were deeply in love, and remained so always. This was part of the secret of his tenderness in the drawing of children, and the agelessness of all his work. Together, and at first with little enough money, they created a supremely happy home.

The wedding was on 28 June 1894 at St Thomas's Church, just round the corner from the bride's home in Manchester Square. The church has long since been demolished, for the parish lost its resident population as private houses were converted to professional or office use, or pulled down to make way for shops.

Their honeymoon was spent in Dorset and Somerset, and, as on all holidays before and after, Leslie took his sketching materials with him. Most of his green watercolours of the English countryside started as holiday sketches. On his first day in any new place he would go out to look for a subject which caught his fancy, and if time or weather did not allow him to complete the picture he would bring it home and finish it in his studio. One landscape at least he started and completed on their honeymoon, a watercolour of the Quantock Hills. Of this his wife used to say that when sketching he was less concerned than she by the proximity of an amiably interested bull.

They came home to 1, Scarsdale Villas, a small house which they rented at the end of a terrace built about 1850 in a quiet South Kensington road, with a room in the back garden which could serve as a studio. In this house a year later their first child was born. At his christening in St Mary Abbots, Kensington, he was given the

Sketch of a calf, 1910

names Leonard Stopford, after his two grandfathers. He was normally known as Leonard, though at an early stage his father nick-
named him Jim, and he always remained Jim to his father, but to no
one else, for the rest of his life.

His mother was slow to regain strength after the arrival of her
firstborn, and the doctor advised that she probably ought not to risk
having any more children, at any rate for the time being, a grievous
disappointment and setback to parents who were as fond of all
children as they were. She tired easily, and found that she could not
walk far, whereas her husband loved walking, and when he was in
the country relished covering long distances at all times of year.
Leonard was a delicate little boy, who might well not have survived
the cold winds and foggy London air but for the care and love with
which they cherished him. He meant everything to them both.

Meanwhile, Leslie Brooke embarked on planning the production
of his first book for children, encouraged by Frederick Warne and
Company, who were one of London's leading publishers of children's
books. His idea was for an extensive collection of nursery rhymes,
old and not so old, with black-and-white illustrations in the text.

Warne liked the proposal, but were conscious of the risk involved for them in producing what would clearly be a substantial book illustrated by a relatively obscure young artist. It would make all the difference if a well-known name could be associated with it. Thus it was that *The Nursery Rhyme Book* came to be published for Christmas 1897 'edited by Andrew Lang, illustrated by L. Leslie Brooke'. Andrew Lang's contribution was to write a pleasant preface, and some historical notes at the end. It was Leslie Brooke who actually settled the general style of the book and selected the rhymes to be included.

This was his first endeavour at book illustrations aimed at very small children, and therefore needing to be full of fun. He knew by instinct that children like to discover details in a picture which at first they have missed, and which perhaps the grown-ups will never notice. His drawing of the crooked man finding a crooked sixpence against a crooked stile, who bought a crooked cat which caught a crooked mouse, contains everything, including an indication of the circumstances in which he bought the cat; but the mouse needs looking for.

How did good King Arthur manage to escape observation when he stole three pecks of barley meal to make a bag-pudding? Leslie Brooke's picture explains, because as the King comes out of the main door of the mill with the barley meal under his cloak, the miller can be seen on the road in the background, chatting to the knight-at-arms on horseback who is possibly asking the way.

Why did Humpty Dumpty, who was in military uniform but carrying an eggspoon in place of a sword, come to fall off the wall? The old nursery rhyme gives no clue, but children are interested in why things happen, and Leslie Brooke's drawing ascribes it to the attentions of a large bee, which flew away after being the cause of the most smashing fall in history.

The lion and the unicorn had evidently had a big fight before the people sent them out of town with their rations. Scrutiny discloses a plaster on the unicorn's nose, while the lion is wearing the ribbon of the Order of the Garter—which presumably he acquired along with the Crown—as a bandage over his left eye. The sharp point of the unicorn's horn is covered by a protective ball, like the button on

23

Humpty Dumpty (*above*)
There was a crooked
man (*below*). Both
from *The Nursery
Rhyme Book*

When good King Arthur ruled this land,
He was a goodly King:
He stole three pecks of barley-meal,
To make a bag-pudding.
From *The Nursery Rhyme Book*

a fencer's foil. If the rules required him to wear this throughout the fight, the lion's success is understandable.

In the picture where 'Four and twenty tailors went to kill a snail', needless to say all the twenty-four are discernible, though any child or grown-up who on a first count can find more than twenty-two is doing well. The drawing of the Five Pigs likewise responds to study. The newspaper which the pig who stayed at home is reading is *The Evening Sty*. Beside his chair are the *Truffle Times* and *The Grunta*. Among the papers strewn on the floor are *The Square Root* and *Tail Twisters*, and, sure enough, the pig who is eating his bit of meat has his curly tail twisted round the back of his chair as a security measure. On the curtains is an acorn pattern, and a picture half-hidden behind them is entitled 'Circe'. Parents who have forgotten the story of Circe would do well to refresh their memory, for they are sure to be asked about it as soon as their children can read. They will have less difficulty over a book half-open on the floor, which is entitled *The Bacons—Their Lives and Litters*.

The drawing at the back of 'This is the House that Jack built' contains a rare and charming compliment by one children's artist to another, his senior. A mother, who looks remarkably like Mrs Leslie Brooke, is showing a picture book to her three children gathered round her, and the book is unmistakably Randolph Caldecott's *The House that Jack built*.

Now that Leslie Brooke had brought out a children's book of his own, he found himself in greater demand from publishers. Dent commissioned him to illustrate a little book described on the title page as '*A Spring Song*, by T. Nash, now again published with sundry pictures by L. Leslie Brooke, 1898'. With much charm they idealise country life, and the pictures are reminiscent of Kate Greenaway. In the same year he illustrated for Duckworth an edition of *Pippa Passes*, by Robert Browning, with seven full-page pen-and-ink drawings which proved his range, for they were as strong, not to say dramatic, as the coloured vignettes in *A Spring Song* were pretty.

The following year saw the appearance of *Singing Time*, a child's song-book in collaboration with his friend Arthur Somervell, later to become Sir Arthur Somervell. A note records that 'all the music in this book has been written out by A.S. and the words of the songs

Lambs frisk and play,
from *A Spring Song*
by T. Nash

and other lettering by L.L.B.' Each of the nursery songs was headed
by a black and white drawing for children to enjoy. The black dog,
which climbs on a small boy's back when he is in a temper, can just
be detected as in ghostly fashion he 'flies like lightning through the
door'; the outburst is over and faces are happy again.

Leslie Brooke developed a special interest in good lettering, as an
artist should. In each of his successive homes, one of his first actions
was to design his own notepaper heading and have it engraved for
daily use. Not unconnected with his care about lettering was another
art-form which he practised with success and enjoyment, the making
of bookplates. A bookplate must aim at catching the outlook, interests, pursuits and achievements of a person, within a small space,
which must be fully used but not overcrowded. His fastidious drafts-
manship, his skilful positioning and his untiring humorous imagination equipped him well.

He first tried his hand at bookplates before he was thirty. He preferred designing them for people he knew well. One of his earliest, and some think his best, was done in 1892 for his cousin who was to become his father-in-law, Stopford Augustus Brooke. It was Stopford Brooke himself who, when seeing a first proof, pointed out that *Ex Libris* must be followed by the genitive case, so 'Augustus' could not be right. This meant that Leslie needed to paint out the final '-*us*' and alter the word to *Augusti*. At least one art critic, whose Latin was hazier, imagined Stopford Augusti Brooke to be the subject's name.

Another of his early bookplates was for his brother Henry. A deep affection between these two lasted all their lives. Leslie was always Tadger to Henry, and indeed in due course to his brother-in-law Graham Balfour also. As a birthday present Henry gave Leslie one year a new shaving-brush, accompanied by the apt couplet 'None but the Badger shall lather the Tadger'. Readers of Dickens may recollect that in *Pickwick Papers*, chapter 33, there is reference to a 'little man in dark shorts who answered to the name of Brother Tadger'. He attended a meeting of the Brick Lane Branch of the United Grand Junction Ebenezer Temperance Association, at which he was accused (falsely) by Brother Stiggins of being drunk, was punched on the nose, and was knocked head first down a ladder. No one ever implied that Leslie Brooke shared the habits or characteristics of Brother Tadger. It was just a friendly sociable name.

Both Henry and Leslie were ardent fishermen, though Henry, who never married, found more opportunity for the sport than Leslie. The bookplate depicts a young man sitting in a meadow by a stream and reading; the family motto was *Ex Fonte Perenni*—from a never-failing spring. Below is the Latin tag, *Pereunt et Imputantur*— they perish and are scored to our account. The word *Pereunt* is encircled by little fish, the word *Imputantur* by the fine fish into which they have grown in the course of the telling.

The Nursery Rhyme Book earned gratifying reviews and sold well from the start, in both Britain and America. It long continued to do so, partly because, being designed for reading aloud to quite small children and being composed of rhymes which were already old, it did not date and did not lose its appeal. It helped to establish a

Bookplates designed by
Leslie Brooke, for his
father-in-law, Stopford Brooke,

and for his brother Henry

reputation for Leslie Brooke as an artist of masterly penmanship who understood the reactions of children through sheer love of them.

The next children's book for him to illustrate was suggested by his publishers, Frederick Warne. Edward Lear's *Nonsense Songs* had been known to the public for a quarter of a century, but Lear, in Warne's words, 'had, contrary to his usual custom, presented these songs to the public illustrated in the slightest manner only'. The proposition was that they should appear in a new edition with illustrations in colour and black and white by Leslie Brooke.

This was a challenge. The verses are exceedingly funny and nonsensical. The pictures had to be realistic (else they would not illustrate), but they also had to be no less funny. The first volume, entitled *The Pelican Chorus*, came out in time for Christmas 1899; the second, *The Jumblies*, twelve months later, and the two were bound together in '*Nonsense Songs*, by Edward Lear, illustrated by L. Leslie Brooke'.

The illustrating of nonsense rhymes presents unusual difficulties. The Jumblies, for example, must be given their own character, over and above the one known fact that their heads are green and their hands are blue. So must the Dong with the Luminous Nose. Edward Lear describes the making and the affixing and the illumination of the nose, but despite its luminosity we are left in the dark as to what a Dong is—except that he is somebody capable of falling in love with a Jumbly girl. Leslie Brooke portrays the Dong as a being of genuine mystery and genuine pathos, and, incidentally, far larger than a Jumbly. He so firmly establishes the character of the Dong that one can hardly imagine a Dong looking other than as he here appears.

The Pobble who has no Toes is another unusual character. Of him we only know that he had a human aunt, named Jobiska, that he was capable of swimming the Bristol Channel, and that he liked to eat eggs and buttercups fried with fish. For identification Leslie Brooke gives him a unique profile, so that again it becomes difficult to conceive any Pobble looking markedly different from this. His colour plate of the Pobble swimming between two ships of the line of olden days is among the most striking of all his picture-book illustrations. No wonder the cherub who is the figure-head on the

And they bought a Pig,
    and some green Jack-daws,
And a lovely Monkey
    with lollipop paws,
And forty bottles
    of Ring-Bo-Ree,
And no end of
    Stilton Cheese.
From *The Jumblies*

and Mrs Discobbolos,
n *The Pelican Chorus*

prow of another vessel turns his head aside from his wooden duty of blowing a trumpet, to take a look at the strange creature in the sea below, whose scarlet flannel still protects his nose, so the toes are not yet gone.

Then there was the Aged Uncle Arly who after visiting the Tiniskoop Hills afar came back at the last to Borley-Melling, where on a little heap of barley he died, mourned by the ever faithful cricket who forty-three years earlier had landed on his nose. The cricket can be seen twice, first when about to jump out of the brambles to its lifelong perch, and at the end in the full panoply of Victorian mourning wear.

The Owl and the Pussy Cat, of course, has passed into English literature. Sundry artists have attempted its illustration. Leslie Brooke in his interpretation makes the owl flirtatious, the pussy cat coy, and the pig a delight.

IV   Johnny Crow's Garden

In September 1899, when the drawings for *The Pelican Chorus* were complete and those for *The Jumblies* were in progress, the Brooke family moved house. Their doctor insisted that Mrs Brooke ought to live in the country. Ever since the birth of her son Leonard in 1895, she had never properly regained her health and strength, and medical advice was that her best chance of doing so would be by getting out of London's smoky atmosphere (far worse then than now) into good country air. Leonard, four years old, would be sure to benefit too.

It was a setback for Leslie Brooke. He liked London, and his professional hopes were centred there, as were most of his artist friends. But it would not have been like him to let any of his own feelings weigh in the balance against the health of his wife and son. They found a house in the village of Harwell, then famous only for its cherries, the best in England. It was fifty miles from London and about a dozen from Oxford, with an excellent train service to both from Didcot Junction; but Didcot was two miles from Harwell, so that to reach the station required either a bicycle or the hiring of a horse and trap, unless there were the time and the energy to walk. True, there was a carrier's cart, but it was before the days of cars and country buses, and indeed of telephones; if one wanted to arrange or re-arrange anything at short notice, to send a telegram was the only way.

The house, of brick with a slate roof, had been built in 1852, shortly after a serious fire had destroyed many of the thatched cottages and farm buildings in the village. Until 1899 it had been a small farmhouse. Leslie Brooke converted the barn into his studio, and the pigsties into potting-sheds. Two pillars by the front door had given it the name of Pillar House, though the Brookes never

33

used that name because they disliked it, thinking it a bit pretentious; and the village was so small that everybody knew where everybody else lived, and there was no necessity for house names anyway.

House and garden and orchard occupied a space of about an acre, and it is this garden which has the prime right to be called Johnny Crow's Garden, because it was here that Leslie Brooke was living when he drew the pictures for that, his best known book. Not that any part of the Harwell garden was recognisable in any of them. A lion and a bear would have found it unduly small. The garden in which Johnny Crow entertained was entirely the product of the artist's imagination.

Artistically, the first-fruits of the move to Harwell were a set of black-and-white drawings for a book called *Travels Round our Village*. This was a simple account of Berkshire village life at the turn of the century, which acquired permanent interest from the chance fact that it was one of the last contemporary writings to portray English

Willum and Jimm
an illustration to
*Travels Round our
Village*, 1901

village people and their thoughts and ways and doings as they were immediately before the isolation of that slow-moving life came to be transformed by the irruption upon it of the car and the country bus.

The author, Miss E. G. Hayden, lived in the small village of West Hendred, a few miles from Harwell towards Wantage. Factually, therefore, West Hendred was 'Our Village', but the drawings were based on sketches Leslie Brooke made not only there but also in Harwell and several of the neighbouring hamlets, and some of the buildings and backgrounds are recognisable still, if one knows where to look. His characterisation of village types was careful and kindly; and though the life changed radically in the next half-century with

Where the Daffodils grow, from *Travels round our Village*

There is Panſies, that's for thoughts

Another illustration from *Travels Round our Village*

the breakdown of the old isolation of the village, the characters are still to be found, and their ways of speech.

About 1901, when Leslie Brooke and his wife had gone up to stay in London for a few days, he called in on his publishers to discuss points concerning his picture-books. They expressed special pleasure that he had come, because there was a separate matter on which they wanted to seek his advice. They were acquainted with an artist and author not previously published by them, who had left with them some coloured drawings for a children's book in the hope that they would publish it. Producing a picture book by a new artist whose name is not familiar to the trade was then, and still is, something of a gamble, and can be an expensive one. In this case, the partners in Warne were divided in their views, and the only course on which they could agree was to ask Mr Brooke. His knowledge of children's reactions to drawings was trustworthy to the point of infallibility, and what he recommended they would do.

Wisely, he said that they must give him time. Might he take the drawings with him, so that he could go through them quietly with his wife? He would bring them back tomorrow. This was agreed to. That evening the two of them went through the drawings together, and the next day he came back with the unhesitating opinion that Warne should go ahead and publish, and the book would be a success. It was. The at that time unknown artist was Beatrix Potter,

36

and the coloured drawings which Leslie and Sybil Brooke pored over together that evening have come to be enjoyed and loved by millions of children and grown-ups all over the world, for they were the coloured pictures for *The Tale of Peter Rabbit*.

In the issue of *Punch*, the weekly London magazine, for 1 October 1902, appeared a small drawing with the initials L.L.B. to which there is a pleasant story attached. A duck wishes to cross a stream. Scorning the obvious path that leads down to the water's edge, the duck prefers to waddle along a nearby wooden plank which spans the water, and saves her from getting her feet wet. Below the drawing is no explanatory note; just the one word, 'Civilisation'.

A few days later, a letter from Paris arrived on the editor's table with a request that it might be forwarded to the artist concerned. This Frenchman's international sense of humour had been so tickled by the joke, that he could not rest without conveying this fact to the unknown Englishman responsible for it. The idea for the drawing amused him; the one-word caption below it captivated him. This chance contact led happily to a friendship by correspondence which lasted many years.

'Civilisation' was not unique; it was one of a series of drawings which L.L.B. did for *Punch* about this time. Indeed he was approached by *Punch* with the suggestion that he might like to become a regular contributor, in the tradition of George du Maurier's

CIVILISATION.

37

weekly 'society' jokes. But he did not fancy this. He recoiled from the prospect of having to be funny to order, every week. Also he knew that his special gift was to make children laugh, not society ladies.

Meanwhile, Leslie Brooke was turning his thoughts to the production of a children's picture book all of his own: a book in which the words would be his, as well as the illustrations. His wife and son, of course, knew of the Johnny Crow game which he and his brother had played with their father on Sunday evenings thirty years ago and more; and it was she who suggested that he might try plaiting together the old Johnny Crow rhymes into a story and call it *Johnny Crow's Garden*.

He liked the idea. So did Warne. He was well enough known now in the children's book world to be able to stand on his own, without need any longer of supporting names from an older generation, such as Andrew Lang and Edward Lear. It would be a test of his originality, too. In the old Johnny Crow game there had been no continuity. Each animal stood alone, in what a later reviewer described aptly as that state of life to which rhyme had called him.

The Lion who had a green and yellow tie on, and the Bear who had nothing to wear, came straight from the old game and were certain claimants for inclusion in the new book. So were others, but it swiftly became apparent that to weave them into a story, or to weave a story out of them, was going to demand the invention of a number of new rhymes too. Some of these were easy enough to compose, but not all. One day Leslie Brooke walked over from Harwell to the village of Blewbury about three miles away, to tea with a friend who lived there, possibly Kenneth Grahame, author of *The Wind in the Willows* and *Dream Days*. On the road back he set himself to find an appropriate rhyme for hippopotamus, to follow after the couplet 'The Stork Gave a Philosophic Talk'. He tussled with it all the way home, and as he reached Harwell the answer came; 'And the Hippopotami said, "ask no further what am I".'

To this the Elephant added 'something quite irrelevant'. Occasionally Leslie Brooke was asked how he came to risk using so difficult a word as 'irrelevant' in a book designed for children. There was no hesitation about his reply. Children are not a bit troubled

Then the Stork
gave a
Philosophic Talk

Till the Hippopotami
Said: 'Ask no further
"What am I"?'

While the Elephant
Said something quite irrelevant

But the Bear had nothing to wear

when they come in a picture book to a word they do not understand, provided that the picture accompanying it is something which they do understand. In this instance they can see that the remark described as irrelevant has obviously annoyed the Stork as much as it has secretly pleased the Elephant. This sufficiently indicates to children the sort of remark it was, and that is all that children want to know. In confirmation, he would sometimes add that he had read *Johnny Crow* aloud to numberless children, beginning with his own boys, and not one of them had ever asked him what 'irrelevant' meant.

Johnny Crow's Garden is dedicated to his two sons. Just as the doctor had forecast, his wife was vastly better in health as a result of moving out of London into the country, and in April 1903 their second child, also a boy, was born. He was christened Henry, after his father's bachelor brother, and indeed Henry had been a Christian

Henry Brooke, 78 years before he
wrote this book about his father

name in the Brooke family for at least six generations. To distinguish them, uncle and nephew became 'big Henry' and 'little Henry' within the family circle, until such time as the passing of years made the latter too obvious a misnomer.

Leslie Brooke now had two children on whom to try out the humour of each of his drawings at the sketch stage. Sometimes, though rarely, it happened that they did not see anything particularly funny in it. In that case there was nothing for it but to scrap and start again. 'Little Henry' had no influence on *Johnny Crow's Garden*, as he was only six months old when it was published, but he had grown to be a powerful and trusted consultant when *Johnny Crow's Party* appeared four years later.

These two books mark the development of Leslie Brooke's skill in bringing into the background of his pictures small points which a child can look for and find, but which many a grown-up might miss. Doubtless this in part explains how the Johnny Crow illustrations have held the imagination and won the love of British and American children in generation after generation.

When the Lion, proud of his tie and with tail erect, is one of the first guests to arrive at the garden door, everyone will see Johnny Crow peeping round the door as he opens it. But not everyone will notice that the latch and the keyhole are not in their normal position but quite close to the ground: at crow-height, that is, not lion-height. Always perfect in courtesy to each of his guests, Johnny Crow in the very next picture has managed to slip an unobtrusive tie round his own neck, so that the Lion may be assured that he has come correctly dressed for the occasion. The Ape, mischievously mimicking the Lion, overdoes it in neckwear.

Members of his family and friends used sometimes to tease the artist with allegations that they could see a strong facial resemblance between some of the Johnny Crow animals and some human relations of his. He staunchly denied that any such resemblance was ever intended—though the evidence to the contrary in one or two cases seems very strong. But part of his genius lay in his ability to draw an animal so that it brought to mind irresistibly a human type. The London tailor, who in those days made suits for him, offered unqualified congratulations on the faces and postures of the

Johnny Crow's guests 'all sat down to their dinner in a row'

three Apes, as one of them took the Bear's measure with a tape, another wrote down the measurements in a large book, and the third laid out a roll of cloth for inspection. They portrayed the expressions of their human counterparts at that moment to perfection, he used to say. Would any member of the medical profession deny that the Goat, who was able to give a reassuring report on the Beaver's suspected fever, had a distinct look of a family doctor at the start of this century, and indeed much later too?

'L. Leslie Brooke' was the artist's normal signature at the end of a letter, and the initials 'L.L.B.' appear somewhere in every one of his book illustrations. But even these three plain initials could be brought in to help the telling of the story. When 'the Pig danced a Jig' they can be seen on a label attached to a branch of a small flowering tree in the background. But when the Hippopotami with their vast bulk and weight gaily decided to emulate the Pig, it is hardly surprising that the label was dislodged.

When the Mouse had built himself a little house, the Cat, who up to this point had hardly entered into the spirit of the day, even to the extent of planning to eat one of his fellow-guests, sat down beside the mat outside the front door to await his victim. Everyone will observe the Mouse's use of the back door to bring in supplies and the sleek Cat shrinking to skin and bone as a result of prolonged starvation. Not everyone will perceive that the passage of time is also recorded by the growth of the grass in front and at the back of the house, and by the 'B' in 'L.L.B.' which has grown a special sprig.

At the end of an eventful day, Johnny Crow's guests 'all sat down to their dinner in a row', and needless to say almost every animal which has been seen taking part in these events can be found sitting on either side of the long refectory table. The only absentees are the Whale, who had been seen leaving early by water, after having driven away in boredom all the listeners to his very long tale except his ever-courteous host, and the peripatetic pair of Penguins who had walked nineteen miles in order to be present. Johnny Crow is seen flying off to them to make sure that they do not miss the dinner. The Lion and the Bear are obviously reconciled, as are the Mouse and the Cat. The Crane, who had been caught in the rain, has a precautionary flannel wrapped round his throat, which lower down

The Three Little Pigs.
Only one troubled to
wave a good-bye to
its mother (*above*)

To deceive the
Wolf this little Pig wok
at four the next mornir
(*below*)

is being tickled by the long feather in the Rat's hat. The poor Beaver, well muffled up, is restricted in his diet to medicine in a wine-glass.

For the following Christmas (1904) Leslie Brooke embarked on fresh seas. He took two of the old nursery stories, *The Three Little Pigs* and *Tom Thumb*, and illustrated them with bold drawings in colour and black and white. Each story was published separately at a shilling (5p). Bound together in stiff boards and entitled *Leslie Brooke's Children's Books*, they were priced at half-a-crown ($12\frac{1}{2}$p).

In these books the purpose of the pictures is to illustrate the letterpress, and there is less opportunity for imaginative humour and bye-plots in the background, but the perceptiveness of the artist is as acute as ever. There was no animal whose facial expressions he could make more of than pigs, as the pictures of the old sow testify when she is sending her three little pigs out into the world to seek their fortunes. Two of them are so pleased with themselves that they walk off without even giving their mother a good-bye glance. It is only the third, the one that outwits the wolf, who turns to wave farewell to her. This is the one also who has a loyal taste in family portraits. Over the wash-stand in his bedroom hangs a portrait entitled **FRIEDRICH BACON**, and over his fireplace and his wolf-skin hearthrug are pictures of his two less prudent brothers.

Tom Thumb in a tip-tilted flower pot.
Family tradition maintains that the author of this book was taken as a model for the little boy

Tom Thumb is a simpler tale, in which the artist has to come to grips with the problem of delineating with sufficient clarity and detail, in a world of otherwise normal size, a small boy who was born no larger than his father's thumb. As Tom is leaning over the edge of the batter pudding which his mother is making, the batter dripping from the spoon she has been using makes a face. On the next page, as Tom falls into the pudding bowl, the batter makes a different and a graver face. The small child who spies Tom hiding in a flower-pot from the King's anger, and subsequently rescues Tom from a royal watering-can, is reputed to have been modelled on Leslie Brooke's younger son, his first appearance in any of the picture books.

A twelvemonth later, this series was completed by the appearance of two further stories, *The Golden Goose* and *The Three Bears*. The first takes place in spring time—for the wild daffodils and bluebells are blooming in the wood. The youngest of three brothers is guided, by a little old man whom he befriends, to a hollow tree, where he finds

The Three Bears at their ablutions

The Great Bear smiles as the
Little Bear misses his target

a goose with feathers of pure gold. Helped by the goose and, more materially, by the little old man, in various adventures and tests, he is eventually granted the hand of the King's daughter in marriage, and in due course inherits the Kingdom, the goose receiving a small crown to wear on her head in recognition of her part in inaugurating the new reign.

The Three Bears is a thoroughly human story. Goldenlocks enters the house of the Great Bear, the Middle Bear and the Little Bear while they are out for a walk, eats up the Little Bear's porridge because she is hungry, sits through the Little Bear's chair because she is too heavy for it, and lies down on the Little Bear's bed and goes to sleep.

She might have guessed that the house was lived in by bears, if she had looked around. On the wall of the room where breakfast is laid out there is a family tree with the family motto, 'Bear and Forbear', and a portrait of a bear in military uniform entitled 'Major Ursa'. The morning paper, not yet unfolded, is *The Bear Truth*; upstairs, above a wash-stand is the precept 'Thyme is Honey—Save it'. At the foot of the Great Bear's bed one can see the constellation called by his name, and the book which the Little Bear has been reading in bed is *Tom Bruin's School Days*.

None of Leslie Brooke's books for children exemplifies better than *The Three Bears* his special power to draw animals which are formidable without being frightening, and whose feelings any child or grown-up can instantly share.

The endpaper of *Leslie Brooke's Children's Books II*, containing the stories of *The Golden Goose* and *The Three Bears*, shows a jester carrying a sandwich-board with the titles of all Leslie Brooke's books up to that date, and lifting a trumpet to his lips. Only those who knew him by sight will have realised that this was a cheery self-portrait of Leslie Brooke jestingly blowing his own trumpet (see page 139).

V Johnny Crow's Party

Meanwhile, *Johnny Crow's Garden* had so successfully established itself, particularly in America, that its author-illustrator began to turn his attention to the possibility of a sequel. Some animals and rhymes which had been considered in 1903 had not in the end been included, and were still available. Some animals, notably the Lion and the Bear, had played such a leading part that they obviously had to be invited again, and new rhymes had to be invented for them. Others, like the Kangaroo, could be made such obvious figures of fun that they deserved invitation on that account alone. Leslie and Sybil Brooke were soon able to compile a long enough list of animals with their rhymes, sometimes with two or three possible alternative rhymes. Then it remained to thread them together so as to create sufficient continuity for a story. The title *Johnny Crow's Party* virtually chose itself.

The pictures in the *Party* are produced by the three-colour process, unlike those in the *Garden*, which were colour lithographs. They may seem to lack some of the gentle atmosphere and beauty of the lithographs, but brightness has probably a stronger appeal to children, whether of that time or this.

The method of work which Leslie Brooke developed was to begin with a rough pencil sketch on transparent transfer paper. Sometimes, though not often, he discarded his first sketch and started afresh. At this stage it was easy to try variations and to alter anything. Artistically he was always a perfectionist, and never satisfied with anything which he thought was good, but not good enough.

When he was convinced that the rough sketch was taking shape as he wished, with the right proportions and the right perspective and the right composition for the space, he would turn the transparent paper over and on the reverse side would draw in, firmly

51

with a soft pencil, the main outlines as they showed through. He would then have his picture as he wanted it, on the back of the transfer paper in reverse.

The next operation was to place the sketch, right way up, on top of a plain white board, and by hard rubbing to transfer to the board the soft pencil outline on the back of the transfer paper. For this stage he normally enlisted the help of his wife. Her part was to hold the edges of the transfer paper, right side up, firmly with the fingers of both hands, while he rubbed over the whole of its surface with some hard object such as the back of a penknife. If the operation went well and the paper did not slip, he would end with sufficient of the soft pencil outline transferred to the white board to enable him confidently to commit himself to drawing over the pencil outlines with pen and indian ink.

This then governed the whole plan of the final composition, providing a framework into which all the subsequent detail could be fitted. Rarely did one of the ink lines need to be altered, but when that happened the faulty part was painted out with chinese white to clear a space for redrawing.

For a colour plate, the outline was patiently and meticulously filled in with water-colour. The black-and-white proofs, when they arrived from the printers, seldom gave much trouble, but with the colour proofs it was a different story. Some illustrators would accept colour proofs which were not absolutely true to the original colours, but never Leslie Brooke. He would take or send them back to Warne, annotated in the margins with small immaculate handwriting, and a line drawn from the note to the place on the picture where the colour reproduction had come out not quite right. 'This should be ultramarine, not violet', 'Bright yellow, not dingy', 'Contrast with adjoining red is too crude' were typical of these marginal comments, blunt but never unsympathetic and phrased with a professional understanding of what the three-colour process at the time could and could not achieve. So the proofs went back to the printers with the artist's criticisms, and revised proofs were anxiously awaited. Generally they came back better, but seldom perfect. Leslie Brooke was not finicky, but he looked for perfection and said so.

'To my nephew Somerset, happy in a name that assures his

TO MY NEPHEW
SOMERSET
HAPPY IN A NAME THAT
ASSURES HIS WELCOME
TO JOHNNY CROW'S – OR
ANY OTHER – PARTY

welcome to Johnny Crow's—or any other—party.' Thus runs the dedication in *Johnny Crow's Party*, and to almost everyone outside the family the second part has been a mystery.

The first four words are simple. Sybil Brooke's only brother Stopford William Wentworth Brooke, always known as Stopford, married an American, Helen Ellis. For some years, to their disappointment, they had no children. It was not until 1906 that their firstborn arrived, and he was christened Somerset Stopford. Why Somerset?

His paternal grandfather, the Rev. Stopford Brooke, married in 1856 Emma Beaumont—whose eldest brother became the first Viscount Allendale. Another brother was Somerset Beaumont, who sat in Parliament as a Liberal M.P. in the eighteen-sixties, but it did not take him many years to conclude that Parliament was not the life for which he craved. A further complicating factor was that he came to regard and admire as the outstanding politician of the time not his own leader, Gladstone, but the leader of the Conservatives, Disraeli, and it was always Disraeli about whom he reminisced. Towards the end of his long life (he died in 1921) he was wont to say that there was only one man of outstanding gifts on the current political stage, Winston Churchill, a perceptive judgment when in most people's eyes at the time Winston's stock stood fairly low.

Somerset Beaumont never married. He lived in a large ungainly house called Hurstcote with an extensive garden in beautiful country

53

near the village of Shere, in Surrey, where he was a generous and lovable if sometimes eccentric host. He made a point of regularly inviting his nephews and nieces to stay, often counting on them to help him entertain his friends and acquaintances who were distinguished in public life.

Throughout childhood and girlhood, Sybil Brooke had each summer spent two or three weeks of holiday there, and after she married the annual invitation came to include her husband and children, so that a stay with Uncle Somerset became an established part of every summer holiday for Leslie and Sybil and their boys. The words in the dedication of *Johnny Crow's Party* were a tribute of gratitude to Uncle Somerset, which was certain to be appreciated and endorsed by all who knew him personally.

In readiness for the party, Johnny Crow had improved his garden, in doing which he invented a practical device for lifting the handles of his wheelbarrow—no easy task for a bird. He had also constructed a maze. The maze, in which the Goose of course got lost, presented something of a problem to the artist too, because he had to devise a maze hard enough for older children not to think it stupidly easy, but not too hard to discourage younger ones from trying to find the way to the centre. A plan of the maze appears in the end-papers of the book, and there is no record of child or parent ever complaining that it was too simple or too difficult. No one could pick up *Johnny Crow's Party* without trying the maze.

When the party began, the Bear in his tailor-made suit sang a sentimental air, which failed to impress his fellow-guests. The Giraffe was inclined to laugh, and even the Duckling couldn't help chuckling.

Not recorded in the text is the behaviour of the Mole, who dug his way to the surface when the singing started, but decided to return underground before it ended. Here one turns back to the previously unexplained frontispiece, which depicts the Duckling meeting the Bear on a path between flower-beds, and trying to sneak past without being noticed.

The Beaver, who on a previous occasion had thought he had a fever, but was cured by Dr Goat who diagnosed the trouble as nothing but his throat, appears to have shown his gratitude by

54

L·G·B·

Johnny Crow Plied Rake and Hoe
and improved his little garden

attaching himself to the Goat as a kind of nursing assistant. He can
be seen in the background helping to roll a bandage with which to
attach the much bruised Snake to a straight stick fitted as a splint.
The Snake's accident had been so violent that even the teeth of the
rake in which he got entangled had been twisted.

Meanwhile the Kangaroo, who was the mischief maker of the
party, had found a tin marked BLUE in the shed where Johnny
Crow kept his garden tools and wheelbarrow. This put into the
Kangaroo's mind the unhappy idea of trying to paint the pink roses
blue, till the Camel unwisely drank the paint. The Elephant, who
had been playing croquet in the background with the Reindeer and
the Hippopotami, rectified the situation by first seizing the Kangaroo's right ear with his trunk and swinging him round at trunk's
length, and then filling his trunk with water which he cascaded over
the suffering roses. The Kangaroo's ear took longer to recover than

And the Kangaroo
tried to paint
the roses blue

Till the Camel
swallowed the Enamel

The Hen said:
'We'll never
come again
To Johnny Crow's
Garden'

the Camel's digestion. Two of the discarded croquet mallets were picked up by the Chimpanzee, who joined in the final vote of thanks to Johnny Crow by banging them on the Elephant's head. The Elephant appears totally unaware of being made a participant in this unusual method of applause.

And before they went their several ways
They all joined together
In a Hearty Vote of Praise
Of Johnny Crow and his Garden

VI   Stories for Children

Leslie Brooke was now forty-five, and the originality of his two Johnny Crow books had secured him a reputation in the ranks of the illustrators of children's books, a reputation which he never let slip. *Johnny Crow's Party* was followed two years later by *The House in the Wood*, a collection of fairy stories translated from the German, somewhat in the style of *The Golden Goose Book*, but for slightly older children who could read stories for themselves. It contains some of Leslie Brooke's most careful and sympathetic drawings, but there is something missing in the stories chosen, and that is the sense of fun. His book illustrations throve on fun. There is plenty of natural fun in nursery rhymes, in Lear's poems, in Johnny Crow, and in the stories of *The Three Bears* and *The Three Little Pigs*. *The House in the Wood* contains ten excellent stories, but there is nothing of carefree nonsense in them. Also there are no pigs.

He proved however that he could draw goblins and make them full of humanity too. *The Goblin and the Grocer* is another simple tale, but his black-and-white drawings of the Goblin raise it to a new emotional level when he is trying to make up his mind in the choice between the student, who had the magical book, and the grocer, who had the jam.

This was Leslie Brooke's last published experiment in illustrating prose stories for children. All the books which followed were based on rhyme, rhyme which was light-hearted or was made light-hearted by his pictures. Only at the very end of his life did he turn to illustrating a prose story again; but that was a nonsense story, and barely half of the black-and-white drawings for it were completed before he died.

Meanwhile, after nine years of happy village life at Harwell, Leslie and Sybil Brooke began to make plans to move their home

Which is it to be?

back to London again. Her health had been the cause of their leaving London in 1899, but there was no longer anxiety on that score. At Harwell they were outside the artistic life of London and cut off from many of their friends, in days when only wealthy people possessed cars—and artists are not wealthy. They were more conscious in 1908 than when they had first taken the house at Harwell that it lacked modern amenities. Water had to be pumped by hand from a well, which in rainy weather used to flood the cellar. Lighting was by oil lamps and candles; there was no gas or electricity. It was hard to keep the house warm in winter, and still harder to warm the studio, which was a converted barn.

In addition, plans had to be made for their younger son's schooling. Leonard, when he was ten, went as a boarder to a boys' preparatory school, Packwood Haugh in Warwickshire. For Henry when he was four it was arranged that a twenty-one-year-old girl, Kathie Hazel, daughter of a retired naval captain who lived nearby, should cycle over in the mornings and give him lessons. He was

59

'*Le rat qui court,*' from a sketch at Harwell

devoted to her, and in later life maintained that nobody had ever taught him better. But this arrangement could not go on for ever.

The upshot was that the Brookes bought the lease of a semi-detached house in St John's Wood, built about 1840. Uncle Somerset's generosity enabled them to add on a studio with a good north light, though it meant sacrificing most of the small back garden. This became their home from 1908 to 1921. They had electricity put in, so that for the first time in their married life they could switch the light on at the door, and not be dependent on lamps that needed lighting. In January 1910 Henry started at Arnold House, a preparatory school about half a mile away for boys between five and thirteen, which had been founded not long before by a remarkably gifted headmistress, Miss Hanson. She became a lasting friend of the whole family.

Back in London, the Brookes were able to pick up links with many of their old friends, one of whom was G. F. Hill, head of the Department of Coins and Medals at the British Museum. He amused himself in his spare time by writing light, semi-nonsense verse, and the thought sprang up that Leslie Brooke might illustrate some of these stories-in-rhyme and make a book of them. Warne approved of the idea and were willing to publish it. Thus *The Truth about Old King Cole* saw the light.

There is no lack of fun here. The stories are new and gay, and the rhyming is skilful. It is, however, almost the only one of the Leslie Brooke books which has visibly dated. Johnny Crow is timeless, as are virtually all nursery rhymes, but Old King Cole 'drove a motor-bus, got up in a gorgeous style, called Vanguardgeneralunionjack, from Putney Heath to the Zoo and back, and charged a pound a mile'. So the frontispiece pictures a London motor-bus of 1911 vintage. It is called Vanguardgeneralunionjack because this combines the names of the three principal companies which pioneered the London motor-bus of the early twentieth century. Each of these names therefore, printed on the side of the bus, was familiar to London children of that generation. Subsequently the London General Omnibus Company ousted the other two, until it in turn was merged into the London Passenger Transport Board, which eventually passed into public ownership as London Transport.

The scene of the frontispiece is the corner of Oxford Street and Orchard Street (note the fruit blossom behind the signpost), where Selfridges now stands. Old King Cole keeps his golden crown in place with a motoring veil such as ladies wore in those days to prevent their hats blowing off. The secret behind Child's Hill, amended to Child's Well, is that Child's Hill, then but not now on the outer edge of London, was the terminus of the bus service that passed nearest to the Brookes' house in St John's Wood. One of the King's three fiddlers can be seen playing to the children; the other two seem to have missed the bus.

Jack and Dick, to whom the book is dedicated, were the author's nephews. He leaves the reader in some doubt as to which code of football it was wherein the King excelled, but the illustrator comes down firmly in favour of the round ball and not the oval one.

Two of the other poems contain reference to 'the Museum'. This is plainly the Natural History Museum at South Kensington, which will have been especially familiar to the author because it was at the time administered jointly with the British Museum in Bloomsbury, and to the illustrator because he visited it to study the appearance and the structures of animals which he could not sketch live at the London Zoo.

But if some of the words and pictures date inescapably to the London of 1911, there is a pair of black-and-white drawings which to the child are deathless. Joe Rumbo, an elephant, had been given by his unkind keeper a currant bun laced with cayenne pepper. 'When he first began to sneeze, he sneezed for half a day.' At the top of the page he stands on his hind legs, preparing to sneeze, with his trunk curled up above his head, and his tail at the back curly too. In the lower part the sneeze comes. His long trunk goes straight out in front, as straight as a gun-barrel; and his tail at the back loses all its curl.

A few years after *The Truth about Old King Cole* came out, G. F. Hill had a knighthood conferred upon him, and became Sir George Hill. It must be admitted that this was not in recognition of his writing of children's verses, but of his being promoted to the top post in charge of the whole of the British Museum.

The summer of 1911 was the hottest and driest in England for

" A - A - A - A - A

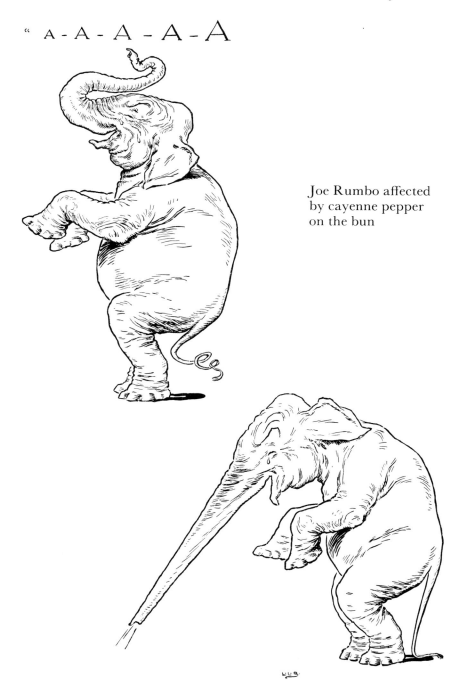

Joe Rumbo affected
by cayenne pepper
on the bun

many years. The Brooke family holiday used to follow a regular pattern. Schools broke up at the end of July, and early in August they would go by invitation of Uncle Somerset for ten days or a fortnight to stay with him at Shere. From there they would go on for two or three weeks on their own, sometimes to the seaside but more often to some farmhouse in the country which let rooms.

That August, gorse and bracken were tinder dry. Shere Heath caught fire and most of it was burnt black, a sad calamity for children whose playground it had been year after year, until they knew every bush and every path across it. The same was true of its near neighbour Albury Heath, twenty years later to be the scene of the fair which was the inspiration of *A. Roundabout Turn*. Fortunately the blackness was short-lived, for within a few days new fronds of bracken were peeping up and preparing to turn the colour of the ground back from black to green again. But when all the gorse bushes and all the young trees had been transformed into black skeletons, what use are they for hide and seek?

The rest of that summer holiday was spent in a farmhouse at Chedworth, a lovely unspoilt village in Gloucestershire, built of Cotswold stone. The journey there was made of course by train. Cars were so rare in the country that the Brookes noticed only one car in the village during the whole of their stay. The railway, built about thirty years earlier, created added excitement because it ran in a cutting through the farm, and one had to cross over a private bridge to reach the farther fields. It would have been an ideal spot on a hot day for boys to sit and watch for trains; but the trains were too infrequent.

Leslie Brooke's two sons were sixteen and eight by now. Despite the difference in age, they were very fond of one another and on holiday did many things together. They both declared it the happiest summer holiday they had ever had, and the sun was a big contributor to its success. Although the elder was not interested in cricket, the younger was cricket-mad. So their father asked the farmer if he could mow the grass for a cricket-pitch in one of the fields beyond the railway, and there at the age of forty-eight he played single-wicket games with his son aged eight for hours and hours. Not until thirty years later, when the son had two boys of his

PLATE I A summer evening, near the Wye Valley

PLATES 2 and 3 Two examples of Leslie Brooke's
detailed comments on colour proofs. (*Above*) Even the
Duckling couldn't help chuckling – from *Johnny Crow's Party*
(*Right*) The Eagle looked quite regal – from the same book

The purple is excellent. The eagle astonishingly good.
The relative darkness of the leaves in the left corner (and browns on bear) makes that part a little out of tone

The shadows on the lion's face are too red — too like the eagle's.

PLATE 4 The Dong with the Luminous Nose

PLATE 5 Old King Cole drove a motor bus got up in a
gorgeous style – from *The Truth about Old King Cole*

PLATE 6 The Lion and the Unicorn were fighting for the Crown
from *Ring O' Roses*

PLATE 7 (*Left*)
Wee Willie Winkie
from *Ring O' Roses*

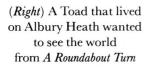

(*Right*) A Toad that lived
on Albury Heath wanted
to see the world
from *A Roundabout Turn*

PLATE 8 Leonard Stopford Brooke, 1895–1918

own, did he realise the full extent of his demands upon his father's time and energy. Fortunately Leslie was always fond of games; indeed, he was well into his sixties before he played his last game of tennis.

As usual on the first morning of a holiday in a new place, he went out with his sketch-book and sketching stool to look for a viewpoint for a water-colour. This year he found, close by, just what he wanted, and time and weather enabled him to complete it before the holiday ended, instead of having to take it home and finish it in his studio. It has lived on as a visible souvenir of an exceptionally happy holiday, as has also a snapshot of the eight-year-old, who, with the farmer's assistance, is riding a cow.

It was a true holiday, for before leaving home Leslie Brooke had just completed the drawings for his 1911 book. This time he took an old rhyme to illustrate, *The Tailor and the Crow*, which concerns a crow, a tailor and a sow. The choice was not a random one. As has been said, there was no animal he drew with more expression than a pig, and there was little that the author and illustrator of *Johnny Crow's Garden* did not know about crows. As to the tailor, it goes almost without saying that he visited a tailor's workshop to study and sketch the posture of a tailor sitting cross-legged on his table to 'shape his cloak'.

Ever since boyhood Leslie had enjoyed walking in the country, and after the return to London he missed the field paths and the open downland. There was also his son Henry needing exercise, for his school had no playing fields of its own nearby. So father and son developed the habit of going out by train for a walk in the country on Saturday afternoons. Instead of taking materials for a picnic with them, they generally stopped somewhere for tea on the way back to the train.

One day on a walk that was new to them both they came upon a cottage which advertised teas in the garden. They went in, found chairs and a table, and ordered tea and bread and butter and jam. Then, while the food was coming, Leslie Brooke took out his sketch book and did a quick pencil sketch of a tree in the orchard. This rough sketch became the pattern for the tree on which the crow took up its baneful perch and enraged the tailor.

65

Watching a tailor shape his coat,
from *The Tailor and the Crow*

The tree and the tea were by the roadside near what was then the village of Kenton in Middlesex. Not many years later Kenton became engulfed in the outward spread of the London suburbs, and the tree and the garden can no longer be found.

In the book, the tailor appears to have had a small house and an orchard on the edge of a country town. The sow evidently had the run of the orchard, when she was not shut into her sty. Unhappily she was shut in there when the tailor shot with his bow and arrow at the excruciating crow. The crow ducked just in time,

'Wife, bring brandy in a spoon
For our old sow is in a swoon'

but with the spent arrow he shot his own sow quite through the heart.

The tailor's compassion shows on his face. He calls to his wife to fetch brandy, while he holds the sow's foreleg as though to feel its pulse, and then cuts a strip from his cloak material to serve as a bandage and hold a pad in place over the wound. The brandy bottle, which has to be searched for, is found hiding inside the grandfather clock. Though hardly the obvious prescription for a damaged heart, it effects a remarkable cure. The weeping small boy, whom his mother embraces and tries to comfort, sees with joy before she does the first signs of miraculous recovery in the animal. The crow, who seems from the endpapers to have been on reasonable terms with the sow originally, flaps away to some less troublous perch.

Following on *The Tailor and the Crow*, Leslie Brooke decided to repeat the pattern which had been successful with *The Golden Goose Book*: that is, to produce a series of four separate, uniform inexpensive books for children in strong paper covers, which could also be bound together in pairs, and ultimately all four could be combined in one substantial cloth-bound volume. To the artist and the publishers this brought the advantages that the drawings to make four books would produce seven, and that they would sell at different prices to suit different pockets.

This time, instead of reverting to prose tales as in *The Golden Goose Book*, he stuck to well known nursery rhymes. The titles of the first two books were *The Man in the Moon* and *Oranges and Lemons*, and these were bound together into *A Nursery Rhyme Picture Book*. All three were published in 1913. The series was to be completed with *Little Bo Peep* and *This Little Pig went to Market*, these to be bound together as *A Nursery Rhyme Picture Book No 2*, and all four to be bound into a volume entitled *Ring o' Roses*.

But war broke out in August 1914, and consequently the second half of the plan did not come to fruition until 1922. During the war years the only additions to the list of Leslie Brooke's books for children were three selections from the *Nursery Rhyme Book* of 1897, entitled—not very meaningfully—*Songs and Ditties*, *Rhymes and Lullabies* and *Tales and Jingles*. These were of smaller format than the originals, to economise in paper, and the three were bound together in a volume called simply *Nursery Rhymes*. All four were published in 1916.

The Man in the Moon came down with his dog, of course, and in Leslie Brooke's illustrations the dog is making sure that the remainder of the bowl of cold pease-porridge is not to be wasted. The Man who had Nought, in creeping up to the chimney-pot, lost one of his shoes and, presumably to speed up his getaway, left his hat on the chimney, blocking it and causing the rooms below to fill with smoke.

The finest heraldic picture Leslie Brooke ever painted depicted the Lion and the Unicorn fighting for the crown. This time the Unicorn had no protective button on the tip of his horn, but the Lion won all the same. Fortunately, the contest left no ill-will behind it, and the two contestants shared the white and brown bread and the plum-cake at a picnic by a stile, which was in fact sketched beside the road leading southward from Shere to the neighbouring village of Ewhurst.

Oranges and Lemons opens with a drawing of six frogs playing the traditional children's game which bears that name. The frog which is about to be caught between the linked arms evades capture by jumping right over them. The different expressions on

the faces of all six display over again the skill of Leslie Brooke in portraying human emotion on the faces of living animals, even an animal so unpromising for this purpose as a frog.

As all the King's horses and all the King's men, headed by the King himself, approach the wall on which Humpty Dumpty has climbed by a ladder, in order to watch so fine a procession and wave a flag, no one perceives the imminent tragedy except two young pages who are acting as trainbearers to the King. Subsequently the King's men, dismounted from their watching horses, try to put Humpty Dumpty together again as though he was a jigsaw puzzle: but alas, it defeats them.

The farmhouse in *Baa Baa Black Sheep* is at Flaunden, a village in Hertfordshire where the Brooke family spent a Whitsun holiday in 1912. Tradition has it that Leslie Brooke's younger son Henry was the model for the drawings of 'the little boy who lives down the lane', although Henry was nine years old at the time whereas the little boy looks no more than five. His father all his life used to fill sketchbooks with pencil drawings of people and places, and could turn back to them whenever he wanted a face or a place or an idea for one of his picture books.

The illustrating of children's books did not by any means exhaust Leslie Brooke's versatility. In the years before, during and after the war of 1914–18 he did a considerable number of portraits in black and red chalk. He specialised in this medium. Some were commissioned by friends, some by Oxford colleges, some were within the family. The fees he asked were not high, and the drawings photographed particularly well, which meant that they could be enjoyed by many.

About the year 1911 a handsome young man from Poland studying in London, Count Edward Raczynski, had been given by a friend an introduction to Uncle Somerset, who invited him to stay and greatly took to him. Uncle Somerset conceived the idea of commissioning his nephew Leslie to do a chalk drawing of the young man to be sent to his father in Poland. When the drawing was finished, he admired it so much that he asked the artist if he would do a replica, which he could keep as a permanent reminder of his young foreign visitor.

At Flaunden, a village in Hertfordshire

There was a sequel. In London some fifty-five years later Leslie Brooke's younger son, into whose possession the replica had passed, met the original sitter, who had worked in the Polish Ministry of Foreign Affairs, and from 1934 to 1945 had been Polish Ambassador in London. He remembered the drawing well. His father had prized it highly. But of course when Warsaw was overrun in the war of 1939–45, first by the Germans and then by the Russians, it had been lost. Happily the replica had survived, undamaged and in good condition, and the pleasure was mutual when this was offered to and accepted by the original subject, aged by that time nearer eighty than seventy, but handsome as ever.

For the Brooke family the return to London in 1908 had been a success. They saw more of their friends. Their house in St John's Wood suited them admirably. It was on the slope of a hill, facing west. A railway tunnel ran below the other side of the road, which had discouraged the developers from building or rebuilding houses on top of it; so opposite them the Brookes had an open space which was used as tennis courts. This gave them an asset which few small houses in London at that time had—a distant view over the rooftops, and magnificent sunsets.

They lived economically, for London life was less cheap than Harwell life. The books brought in a modest but steady income; in almost every case the publishers had contracted with the artist to pay him no lump sum or advance royalties, but a flat-rate royalty per copy sold, with no terminal date, the rate being slightly higher for home sales than for export sales (chiefly to America). This he supplemented with commissions which came along for portraits, bookplates, dust-cover pictures for new novels, and occasional illustrations for magazine stories such as *Joseph, a Dancing Bear*, which was published as a monthly serial story in *Pearson's Magazine*. All these were welcome to him, for money was not easy. Neither he nor his wife had much in the way of private means, and they went carefully so that they could afford to give their two boys the education they wanted for them.

In 1912 Henry, the younger, left his day-school in London at the age of nine, and followed his brother to Packwood. Leonard left Marlborough at the same time. It was shortly after his seventeeth birthday, and he could have stayed longer but for medical advice. Physically he had always been a delicate rather than a sturdy boy. Marlborough in those days, with its cold winds over the Wiltshire downs, had the reputation of being a 'kill or cure' school for anybody liable to chest trouble, and the doctor thought that it would be unwise for him to risk another winter there.

He left with mixed feelings. He had never been the sort of boy who really enjoys school life. He was too shy and retiring for that, and he had never been much good at cricket or football, which in those days were compulsory. Swimming was the sport he loved, but this was before the days of heated baths which could be used all the year round.

Neither did he reach distinction in the classroom, though he worked hard. Those were times when public schools were commonly divided into a Classical Side and a Modern Side, with the Classical Side attracting almost all the kudos and the Modern Side being regarded by many as not much more than a receptacle for those who found Latin and Greek too hard for them.

The subject by which he had been enthralled ever since early childhood was History. Had he gone to school twenty years later— by which time its importance as a school subject was widely recognised—he might have found himself in a flourishing History Department, where his enthusiasm and his capacity for hard work when his interest was aroused would probably have carried him high. He exemplified the tragedy in a system of education which did not offer enough options for every keen boy to find the niche that suited him.

He wanted to get to Oxford, and after leaving school it was arranged for him to work with a tutor in London. This was a dreary experience, but it achieved its object, and he was accepted for a place at Lincoln College, Oxford, in October 1914 to read History. To fill the intervening year, he went to live with a French family in the town of Meaux, happily unaware of the part it was so soon to be called upon to play in the Battle of the Marne. He learnt to speak fluent French, while enjoying the opportunity to read widely in literature and history.

At Easter 1914 his father joined him in France for a memorable holiday. Leslie Brooke had learnt good schoolboy French, but in the intervening years had had little opportunity to practise it, except when he and his brother Henry and his sister's husband Graham Balfour had gone off together for short holidays to favourite spots of theirs in the Normandy countryside. Maybe it was his Irish blood which gave Leslie Brooke remarkable imitative powers, both of voice and gesture—when telling Irish stories he could drop into the brogue of several parts of Ireland—and in France his accent and intonation and the movements of his hands constantly led Frenchmen on first acquaintance to ascribe to him greater command of the language than he really possessed. But he was proud to have a son who could make up now for any of his own linguistic limitations.

In the autumn of 1913 Leslie Brooke decided that he would do for the first time what he had often thought of doing; he would design his own Christmas and New Year card to send to his friends. He drew a small youngster in Boy Scout uniform, marked '1914', with the caption 'I wonder if there is somebody I can help'.

On 4 August 1914 Britain went to war with Germany in fulfilment of her long-standing treaty obligation to come to the aid of Belgium if ever she was a victim of unprovoked aggression. The war, it was commonly said in England, would be over in three months; Germany could not hold out longer. In fact, it lasted four years. Britain kept faith with Belgium, and she and her allies overwhelmed the Kaiser's Germany in the end, but not before untold suffering had been inflicted on vanquished and victors alike. The aftermath of his 1914 New Year card was too poignantly terrible for Leslie Brooke ever to try another.

VII   Years of War

Leonard had just passed his nineteenth birthday when war broke out, and like almost every young man of his age and upbringing he volunteered for the Army at once. But he did not pass the doctor. His long-standing chest trouble, which had caused him to leave Marlborough earlier than intended, had not yet gone; and in those early days the rush to join up was such that the Army could afford to defer accepting anyone who was not a hundred per cent fit. The decision disappointed Leonard, but it enabled him to take up his place at Lincoln, and he benefited in more ways than one from his two terms there, although Oxford was but a shadow of its normal self. Numbers were small, and most of the undergraduates were either medical rejects or students from overseas.

In the first few days of 1915 Leslie Brooke's mother died, after a short illness. She was eighty-five, and had been a widow for nearly thirty years. The family business in Liverpool had been sold in 1909, and she and her elder son Henry, who had been managing it since his father's death, moved their home from Merseyside to a flat in London not more than half a mile from Leslie and Sybil. The family had always been close-knit, and this was a wholly happy arrangement for all of them. Leslie's sister and brother-in-law, Rhoda and Graham Balfour, had earlier moved from Oxford to Colwich, a village near Stafford, on his being appointed Director of Education for Staffordshire. Sybil and her sister-in-law had long been the closest of friends.

On Mrs Brooke's death, Leslie and Sybil begged Henry, who was then fifty-four, not to live alone but to come and make his home with them. He was touched by this offer, but firmly declined it, putting their interest above his pleasure. He was that sort of man. He believed profoundly in husband and wife being on their own

A photograph of Rhoda Brooke, Leslie Brooke's mother

and bringing up their children in their own way, with no third party, however dear a friend, intruding. So he obtained rooms not too far away from them, where he could bring his own furniture and have his meals cooked and served by his landlady, an arrangement less difficult to obtain in those days than in these.

On selling what remained of the family business in Liverpool and moving with his mother to London, he had secured congenial part-time work as Secretary to the governing bodies of two of the smaller public schools, which found his integrity and devotion as well as his business experience and exactitude invaluable to them. However, part-time work earns no more than a part-time salary, and he had to live carefully, denying himself many pleasures in order to keep within a limited income. But this did not stand in the way of his being a beloved uncle to his young Brooke and Balfour nephews; and every Sunday morning he would walk back from church to lunch with the Leslie Brooke family, and often go for an afternoon

Chalk drawing of Sybil,
Leslie Brooke's wife, aged 43

walk with them over Hampstead Heath. Between the two brothers, Henry and Leslie, a friendship, close and deep, lasted unbreakably. Their brother-in-law Graham Balfour came within it too, and their sister Rhoda Balfour and Leslie Brooke's wife Sybil instinctively shared all their joys and sorrows and anxieties.

Leslie Brooke was fifty-one years of age when the war broke out, and as it went on he yearned to find some form of war work for which he could offer himself. Throughout his life he kept himself physically fit, but he was too old for military service, and his partial deafness, which for thirty-four years had been slowly but inexorably worsening, shut him out from most of the forms of part-time voluntary service where men of his generation sought to contribute what they could to the war effort. He was riled by his feeling of personal uselessness, and it was not until 1916 that he read of something which he seemed well fitted to do. An appeal was made for volunteers over military age to act as guides to Australian soldiers on leave who expressed a wish to see some of the cultural sights of London, including museums and picture galleries.

Tiny as this contribution might be, it was one which he was exceptionally well qualified to make, where partial deafness was not a disabling liability. At the pre-arranged meeting-place in Central London he would pick up some twenty or more Australian soldiers who had opted through Australia House for such a tour, and after enquiring whether there were particular places which any of them had set their hearts on visiting, he would quickly plan the tour in his mind and lead them off. Those who were genuinely interested were lucky indeed, because he had a natural gift not only for simple exposition but for transmitting his own enthusiasms to others. If there were one or two who showed exceptional interest, as in each group there generally were, he would invite them back for a meal at his house where they could see the studio of a working artist, and come into a family home to continue their conversations and forget the war. In a number of instances this led to lasting friendships among those who survived their ordeal in France and returned safe to Australia.

One day during the war an elderly man called at the door and asked if he could see Mr Brooke. He had with him a quantity of prints from his own wood engravings, which he was trying to sell in order to raise a little money in difficult times. It turned out that he had managed to get the addresses of a number of artists living in and around St John's Wood, so that he could call at their houses. Leslie Brooke, stirred with sympathy for a member of his own profession down on his luck, asked the old man his name. 'Quick— Mr Quick.' 'Not W. M. R. Quick?' The man's face lit up. 'Yes, how did you know?' Leslie Brooke remembered the initials of the engraver from the days when pictures for the illustrated papers were generally engraved on wood, under sharp pressure of time. Then the art of the wood-engraver was supplanted by more modern methods of reproduction, and men like W. M. R. Quick were without a job.

Leslie Brooke was determined to help in some practical way. If he got together a small class, would Mr Quick come along and teach them his art? The old man was overjoyed.

The following week Mr Quick arrived with the tools and the box-wood blocks and the leather sandbags to go beneath them, and he found a class of four awaiting him: Leslie Brooke, his young son Henry and his two fellow-students from old days, Clem Skilbeck and Willie Parkinson, were all willing to be pressed into service. The tools needed to be very sharp. The tutor handled them with the skill and control of a surgeon, and could not understand why the four pupils were so clumsy with them. After an hour or so the class voted for a tea-break. Willie Parkinson, who had enlivened the afternoon with *sotto voce* remarks, said he must wash his hands before tea because they were 'dripping with blood'. Indeed, all the pupils gashed themselves, but the classes continued.

From 1915 onwards there was one ever-present anxiety. In the spring of that year Leonard passed his medical test and was free to join the Army. His schoolboy experience as a cadet in the Officers' Training Corps at Marlborough gained him a commission in the King's Royal Rifle Corps, 16th Battalion, which at the time was training in Essex and later moved to Salisbury Plain. Soldiering was not in his blood. It was a matter of plain and unquestioned duty. He made friends among brother-officers, gained self-confidence and gave of his best. In November 1915 he crossed to France, though he

79

went there not with the K.R.R.C. but with the Army Cyclist Corps, a regiment to which, much to his annoyance, he had been seconded.

To celebrate his twenty-first birthday on 11 July 1916 he could not exactly have a party, for he spent it in the trenches, though his parents had sent him some champagne which miraculously reached him safely. He occupied part of that day in writing a friendly letter to his young brother, about the changed life he would be entering when he started as a new boy at Leonard's old school, Marlborough, in a few weeks' time.

It was not long after this that there came one of those turning points in life, after which nothing is quite the same again. Leonard wrote to his father from France that he had decided to apply for a transfer to the Royal Flying Corps (it had not yet had its name

An experiment in wood engraving

changed to the Royal Air Force). An appeal had gone out for young Army officers to volunteer for flying training. By this stage of the war, aircraft were coming along faster than men able to fly them. He had no previous experience of flying, but that was not called for. He felt that this was something he could do, or at any rate attempt to do, and that by responding to the appeal he might make a more positive contribution to the war effort than he believed he had been able to do up to that time.

His parents accepted his decision without question, but of course could not conceal from themselves that he would be putting his life at greater risk. Aviation in 1916 was still an embryonic science, and it was hazardous to fly at all in the simple aircraft of those days, let alone go into battle in them. Yet they knew that his decision would not have been a careless or a quixotic one, and that it was for them to back him up and to bear their increased anxiety for him with a smile. There was entire understanding between the three of them.

It also meant that, for training as an observer in the first instance, he would have to come back to England. He would be away from the sheer physical discomforts of life in the trenches, and they would see more of him, at any rate until his training was sufficiently advanced for him to be sent overseas again.

Leonard himself never doubted that he had decided right, though he knew what it meant for them. He never faltered or had second thoughts. He found, to his own surprise, that he loved flying. It meant more to him than anything he had had to do in the Army: more, indeed, than anything he had ever done in life. This diffident and unsure boy had discovered, almost by chance, something he could be quite sure about, something which he could do really well.

He completed his flying training, successfully qualifying as an observer, and in due course returned to Northern France, where he found himself mainly detailed for reconnaissance work over the enemy lines. His nerve never failed: he was carried away by the great new adventure of being up in the air, with a job to do.

His next ambition, of course, was to qualify as a pilot, and at the end of 1917 he was sent back to England again for this purpose. He enjoyed life more and more. He grew in his feeling of power over the elements. He was to make a very good pilot. He was selected to learn to fly heavier machines, medium-range bombers. In August 1918 he crossed to France and joined what was named the Independent Air Force, located in Eastern France, concentrating on bombing of targets in Germany far behind the lines. Fully laden, these aircraft took an hour to climb to their operational height of 16,000 feet, and so their airfields could be situated far back deep in the French countryside, out of earshot of gunfire. On non-flying days, it afforded the most peaceful and rural background to the war imaginable.

Daylight bombers were vulnerable and suffered heavy casualties in the First World War as in the Second. On 25 September 1918, Leonard was posted missing. Five weeks later his parents learnt that he had been killed in action. The news reached them nine days before the Armistice was signed and the war ended. On the night of the Armistice Leslie Brooke, controlling the intensity of his grief, took his younger son Henry, then fifteen, to Piccadilly Circus and Trafalgar Square and around central London, because he wanted him to have a memory of the lights and the crowds and the rejoicings to last for the rest of his life. Excusably, people imagined at that time that the war at last ended was a war to end war. But it turned out otherwise.

His parents never wholly got over the tragedy of Leonard's death, coming as it did after years of anxiety, and so close to the conclusion of war. But his father never allowed personal sorrow to affect the quality of his work, and there is no perceptible trace of sorrow in his post-war drawings. His sense of fun was unimpaired when children were around, or when he was drawing for children.

Many of the letters of sympathy which he and his wife received from their closer friends and relations who knew Leonard well made mention of the remarkable development of his personality and inner strength which wartime experience, and particularly flying, had produced in him. One of his former headmasters wrote that of all the boys who had passed through his hands, none had shown so great a transformation of character and confidence and self-possession as a result of going through the war. It pleased his parents that others had shared with them this perception of a deep change in their son, a change wholly for good.

In later years they sometimes speculated what profession Leonard would have taken up, had he been spared. It seemed likely that he might have turned to serious journalism. But it would almost have broken his heart, had he been obliged to give up flying.

Arthur Williams the 'cellist,
said by many to be
the best chalk portrait
Leslie Brooke had ever done

VIII   Children's Books Afresh

Quite early in 1919 Leslie Brooke started to discuss with Warne the practical question of his doing the drawings for two more books of nursery rhymes, *Little Bo-Peep* and *This Little Pig went to Market*. Those would make up the second half of *Ring o' Roses* as originally intended. He had not tried his hand at book illustration while the war was on. In 1917 and 1918 he was receiving a number of commissions for the portraits in black and red chalk in which he excelled. He always liked this work, and particularly so at this time because it filled his whole mind while a sitting was in progress. In that anguished month of October when he did not know whether Leonard was alive or dead, he was engaged on portraits of three young children, and very good portraits they turned out.

Earlier in that year, he had been asked to do a chalk portrait of a well-known 'cellist, Arthur Williams, who had been playing in a quartet in Berlin when suddenly the 1914 war broke out. The Germans interned him immediately at Ruhleben, and he suffered tragically in health from privations there, until eventually he was released and allowed to return to England under an exchange agreement. It was a question whether he would ever regain the suppleness and control of his fingers which professional playing to his standard demanded.

It was desired that the portrait should show Arthur Williams from the left, playing his 'cello, with the instrument therefore in the foreground. It was commonly said to be the best chalk portrait he had ever done. But what drew especial comment from the music-lovers who saw it was the flawless care with which the detail of the 'cello was drawn. They had expected the artist to leave that vague, and not devote much time or trouble to it. But this was not Leslie Brooke's way. With his pen or his chalk he never fluffed anything.

He was asked to draw a musician playing a 'cello, and he would have counted it failure if he had drawn a 'cello which could not be played.

This was indeed one of his principles; an artist must not run away from his problems. Among his friends in later years was a young and more famous artist, who used to beg Leslie Brooke to be frank in criticising his paintings, because he always found something to learn from his criticisms even if he did not agree with them. Leslie Brooke for his part could not understand why so gifted an artist had never bothered to learn the rules of perspective. It was as though a novelist had never troubled to learn to spell. Admiring one of the younger man's new pictures, he would say: 'That cow there. It could never stand up, you know, could it? Is it important to your composition that the cow is bound to fall over? Or is it just that you have not taken enough trouble to draw it right?' They remained firm friends, and the mutual respect grew rather than diminished.

In his black and red chalk style Leslie Brooke was asked to do posthumous portraits of several young men who did not come back from the war. He did not find these easy, particularly if he had had no more than slight acquaintance with the subject. It was hard to deduce character from photographs. Yet for obvious reasons he was more than ordinarily anxious to get it right and to produce a picture that would give satisfaction and pleasure to the family and friends.

Early in 1920 he determined to start on a posthumous drawing of his son Leonard, although he was not at all sure he could succeed. But he did. He never worked more lovingly on anything. By comparison with drawings and photographs of Leonard when he was younger, he brought out tellingly the strengthening of personality and character which the war and flying had brought about. To those who had known Leonard it was completely satisfying, and a noble tribute from a father to a son.

Naturally his parents wished to visit his grave in occupied Germany, as soon as permission from the authorities could be obtained. His aircraft had come down in beautiful wooded country close to the village of Blankenborn near the small town of Bergzabern, only a few miles beyond the new frontier between Germany and France. By August 1920 permission was obtained, and Leslie and Sybil and their younger son set out on a journey which combined sadness with reassurance. They crossed the Channel and travelled by train to Strasbourg, which they made their base. From there they went on to Bergzabern, the terminus of a short branch railway line, and spent two nights in a small hotel.

They had written in advance to the burgomaster, who received them with courtesy and sympathy. He told them that the pilot and his young observer appeared to have both been killed instantaneously in the air. The bodies had been brought down from Blankenborn to Bergzabern, and buried with military honours in the small military section of the town cemetery. There had been no fighting in the neighbourhood, and this seemed to have been the one incident in the whole war which had physically touched that countryside. Though some people in the inn and the town looked askance at the visitors, as ex-enemies—that was inevitable—to the burgomaster they were a sorrowing family and he offered any help that the municipality could give.

So Leonard and his observer, David Provan of Glasgow, aged nineteen, slept in a place of honour, alongside a few soldiers both French and German who had died in the Franco-Prussian war of 1870, on an open hillside above the town, looking over to lovely woods and vineyards. The wife of the cemetery-keeper, full of sympathy, had been keeping these graves tidy, and offered to continue to do so, and to plant them with whatever was wished. Frau Stephan was a good and kind friend with whom the Brookes kept in touch for many years.

Each grave was headed by a wooden cross, bearing an oval metal plate on which was written in German, 'Here rests in God an English airman Leonhard Brooke (David Provan) who fell at Blankenborn near Bergzabern, 25 September 1918.'

A year or two later, Leslie Brooke received a letter from the Imperial War Graves Commission explaining that it would only be practicable for the Commission to guarantee in perpetuity the proper care of British graves in scattered local cemeteries if they were brought in to one or other of the main British cemeteries in Germany for our war dead; and seeking his permission to do this. But after long discussion with Leonard's mother and brother, and consultation with David Provan's parents, who agreed, he decided to say no. They had a personal link now with the place where these two boys fell, and where they had been buried with honour. To move them to some large cemetery might seem an act of almost churlish ingratitude to the Bergzabern community, where their funeral was likely to be long remembered; and as for care in perpetuity, so long as Leonard's father or mother or brother was alive the graves would be cared for, and after these three were all dead, what would it matter? The decision turned out to be the right one, though the final reason which clinched it could not by then have been foreseen.

During the first eighteen months from the end of the war, a succession of chalk portraits occupied most of Leslie Brooke's working time. It was only after the return from Bergzabern, with treasured photographs as well as memories, that he turned again to drawings for children's books and took up the completion of *Ring o' Roses*. He worked more slowly at first, until he was in the swing of it again. But no one could guess, from the quality or feeling of the drawings in this book of nursery rhymes, that half of them had been done nine years later than the others, a world war and a profound sorrow intervening.

Of course, there were new interests to cater for. Small children would constantly climb on his knee and ask him to draw something for them. 'What shall I draw?' Usually it was a horse or a lion or a monkey or some other animal, and this presented no problem. But one day a little boy whose father worked for an oil company said: 'A petrol pump.' This was a novel request and one for which he was totally unprepared. It was a moment for inspiration and fortunately sufficient inspiration came to him, and his petrol pump passed muster.

The work on *Ring o' Roses* coincided with long consideration and discussion of the question whether the Brookes should stay on in London or move to the country again. When they came to 14 Marlborough Hill in 1908 they bought it on a lease due to expire in 1938, so there was no pressure on them to make a move, and it carried for them all the most vivid memories of the war and Leonard's part in it. At first they could not have brought themselves to leave and turn the key on all this; but as the months went on they increasingly thought that happiness was likelier to be regained if they could find a new home which would not every day be reviving poignant memories. Sybil was slow to recover from the deadly shock of losing Leonard, and began to yearn for the healing peace of the countryside and a fresh start. Relations and friends were generous in inviting them to come and stay for a week or two of holiday in the country, to give them a break; and they also found rooms in the village of Cold Ash, near Newbury, some fifty miles out of London to the west, where the kind owner of the house looked after them well, so they had peace from the bustle of a great city.

All this experience convinced them that the right course was to look for a house which they could buy in the country, not too far away from other members of the family and friends. They travelled to visit a number of houses for sale, of which they had information from house agents, but time went on and they saw nothing wholly suitable. They discovered that it was harder to make up their minds on which was the right house when there was half of England to choose from, than if they had been obliged to settle on one within a limited radius.

What brought matters to a head was that in the autumn of 1921 they received a particularly good offer for the unexpired portion of the lease of their house in St John's Wood. They resolved to accept this, partly because it would force them to reach a decision on where they should go to live. At the end of November 1921 they moved out of 14 Marlborough Hill, sending almost all their furniture and belongings temporarily into store. They reckoned that it would be only there three or four months before they could move it out again into their new house, wherever that might be. Their expectations were optimistic, for it remained in store for two years.

On 3 January 1922 Leslie Brooke and his son Henry took a train to Oxford, and the following morning, armed with particulars of one or two houses which were up for sale, went for an exploratory round walk of some ten miles to see the village of Cumnor, returning to Oxford by way of Wootton and Boar's Hill. They did not let themselves be kept away by the gloomy description of Cumnor in a guide-book to the county. 'There are few places in Berkshire more dispiriting and woe-begone than Cumnor. Emphatically it is not "residential". Almost, indeed, does it seem like a hamlet on which a curse has rested, and our little tour to it has been undertaken simply because it was unavoidable. The wise man will not really go there at all.' Neither were they deterred by the unwelcoming north wind which froze them as they walked up Cumnor Hill, nor by the notoriety of Cumnor as the place where in 1560 Amy Robsart was found dead at the foot of a staircase—was it an accident or was it murder? According to local legend her ghost haunted the village for many years, and this grew so serious that ultimately nine divines were persuaded to come out from Oxford and lay the ghost. This they did, and laid her in the village pond, which still exists; and she was never seen again.

Despite all this, and despite each of the houses of which they had been given particulars looking quite unsuitable, Leslie and his son agreed that, if only there were a suitable house for sale there, Cumnor was the sort of village where they might be happy to live.

Indeed, the Brookes were increasingly disposed to concentrate their search on the country around Oxford. They had friends there, including two of Sybil Brooke's sisters and their families. They would feel at home; Oxford had been their nearest town when they lived at Harwell. The train to London took little more than an hour, and it would be easy to go up for the day when they had a wish to do so. In addition, it would mean that for the next four years they would be able to see much more of their remaining son, because in October 1922 he was due to go up to Balliol College, Oxford, as an undergraduate.

They spent much of that year staying in friends' houses or in rooms which they had known and liked before. Leslie was busy completing the final drawings for *Ring o' Roses*, which was to be published in time for Christmas. When these were all done, they planned a short holiday across the Channel, taking with them Leslie's brother Henry, who had suffered a collapse from overwork following on a serious fire at Trent College, one of the two schools which he was responsible for administering. They were determined to take him to some quiet place out of England, where he could rest and no letters or engagements or work could follow him. Their choice fell on Gisors, a small old town in Normandy, involving no long travelling but ideal for someone who loved rural France and was in need of a change of scene and a rest.

By the time they returned to England, Leslie and Sybil were no nearer to finding a house for sale where they would like to make their home. But they had the chance to rent from a friend a small furnished cottage in Cumnor village, for an indefinite time. It was simple enough, but they could fit into it and make it their base until the right answer to their problem came along. It was called Fish-ponds because the rather muddy ponds in the fields at the back were reputed to be the remains of the ponds which in olden days had provided the monks of Cumnor with their fish.

Another friend who lived in a beautiful house of Cotswold stone on the edge of the village began to urge upon them the idea that they might buy a piece of land adjoining her orchard, and build a house there. It would be peaceful, set back from the road behind trees. It could be designed to suit their needs and wishes, and would command a superb open view across the Vale of the White Horse to the Berkshire downs twenty miles away.

To have to build their own house, with all the delay entailed, was the last thing that had entered the Brookes' minds when they decided to leave London. But nearly twelve months of searching for the right house to buy had proved fruitless, and they had no wish to remain homeless for ever. Gradually and reluctantly they came round to accepting the view that to buy this site and build was going to be the most sensible course for them. They would have pleasant neighbours. They were growing to like the village more and more. They would be within five miles of the centre of Oxford, yet surrounded by fields and right outside Oxford's modern suburbia.

There was one other consideration which made it easier to take the decision to build and not to buy. A very few days after the Brookes left their London home Somerset Beaumont (Uncle Somerset) died. He was eighty-five, and had been ailing for some time. It was learnt that he had left his personal effects and belongings and most of his money to be divided between ten nephews and nieces, of whom Sybil was one; and her share would provide her and her husband with, for the first time, some substantial capital behind them.

They had been married for twenty-eight years, and all that time they had had to live thriftily. It came naturally to them that they could not afford extensive entertaining or costly holidays. They could not give their children expensive presents, but they had stinted themselves to give them a good education. Money had been a problem for them, particularly during the war years; but any thought of overspending their income would have horrified them both.

Uncle Somerset's bequest acted as a turning point in their way of life to the extent that it freed them from worry over money. It did not alter their simple tastes, but they could now afford to buy a couple of acres of land, and build the sort of house they desired and plan the sort of garden they wanted. They could have a tennis court made in the garden, and in due course they could buy a car, their first.

Meanwhile they had Fishponds as a temporary home, right on the spot for keeping an eye on the builders, and 1922 was the first Christmas since 1913 to see a new children's book illustrated by Leslie Brooke on the market. *Ring o' Roses* turned out a happy choice of title, and the pictures proved that at the age of sixty he was still as close to the mind and likings of a child as he had ever been. As of old there was plenty of the unexpected in the illustrations, and plenty to look for.

This Little Pig went to Market, six seemingly unconnected lines of verse, turn into drama, with the little pig who had had none of the roast beef finding the little pig who lost his way, and bringing him home to a welcome resembling that of the prodigal son. The tails of the different pigs at the different stages are worthy of study: straight for misery, curly for joy. On the wall is a picture of a sty over the caption 'There's no place like home', and the curtains are decorated with an acorn pattern.

Not everyone has thought to ask why Jack and Jill went up the hill, not down the hill, to fetch a pail of water. Leslie Brooke makes it plain. A short way up the hill was a stream with a small waterfall, ideal for filling pails. Their mother, after bandaging Jack's crown, gave each of them a slice of bread and jam. Jill has bandaged her doll's head, out of sympathy, and maternally feeds the doll with her slice.

Little Bo-peep fell fast asleep under a small tree, and dreamt that

There is no place like home—even for pigs

In the tree, the faces of the lost sheep

she had heard her lost sheep bleating. Had she woken and looked up into the tree above her, she might have spotted the faces of a dozen of them visible among the leaves and branches.

The book ends with a brief rhyme about Wee Willie Winkie, of whom one knows so little apart from his nightly activity at eight o'clock. But Leslie Brooke has given him a character and personality and has created an atmosphere round about him. He once said that he regarded the picture of Wee Willie Winkie listening at the keyhole as the most artistic of all the illustrations he ever did for children's books. Why is he standing at the top of three small steps outside a front door? Because he ran through the town 'upstairs and down-stairs'.

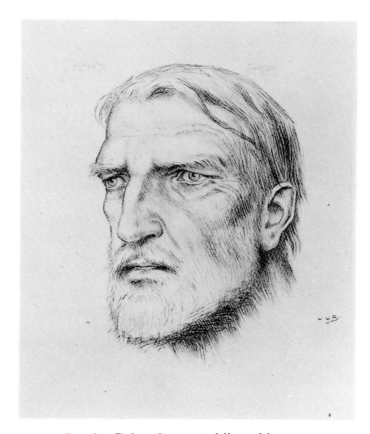

Snarley Bob—the part-philosophic
part-bucolic character in *Mad Shepherds*

A few years before the war Leslie Brooke's brother-in-law Dr
L. P. Jacks, Principal of Manchester College, Oxford, asked him if
he would consider doing a frontispiece for a story he had written
called *Mad Shepherds*. The central figure was a part-philosophic
part-bucolic character called Snarley Bob, and a drawing of him
would, it was thought, help the reader to see this strange and
powerful personality in perspective. So he gave Leslie a summary of
the story, and he responded with a sketch for the frontispiece.

But it was not right. Lawrence Jacks replied with a polite letter of
thanks which left no doubt in Leslie Brooke's mind that he had not
hit the target. He wrote back to say that he would like to have

95

another shot. Would Lawrence let him have the text of the whole story, so that he could read it at leisure and soak it in? This was done, and Leslie perceived at once the inadequacies of his first attempt. He took a great deal of trouble over the second drawing, and sent it off. Lawrence responded with a telegram of congratulations and delight, and anyone who reads the story can easily see why.

Some years later, after the war, Lawrence Jacks and his publishers wanted to bring out a new edition of *Mad Shepherds*, in a larger format, with further pictures. Would Leslie Brooke be disposed to do six or eight full-page black-and-white illustrations? The frontispiece would of course be retained.

The request came just at the time he had finished the work on *Ring o' Roses*. He anticipated that it would be difficult, for Snarley Bob was not wholly of this world, but he thought he would like to try. He read the story again very thoughtfully, and started work. He was living in a village again now, and that helped. The settle in one picture was drawn from a settle in the old inn at Cumnor, the Bear and Ragged Staff; and he had not lived under the Berkshire downs without having chatted with many shepherds. These were, in fact, the last black-and-white illustrations he ever did for a serious book, and each of them took him a long time. But he was pleased with the result, and so were the author and publishers. The new edition of the book appeared in 1923.

IX *Leslie Brooke's Own Garden*

A great part of Leslie Brooke's early years at Cumnor was occupied with creative work far removed from book illustration. For the first time in his life he had the opportunity to plan a house to live in, and a garden in which it would be set. He had an architect of note to design it, Mr (later Sir) Clough Williams Ellis, a friend of the neighbour who had urged him to buy the site. By good fortune the two men got on together excellently, although their ideas of what sort of a house it was to be did not always tally. Leslie Brooke wanted one with plenty of wall space to hang pictures. Clough Williams Ellis said that on the whole he preferred rooms without pictures, though he granted that an artist must have some space for pictures somewhere.

All these differences were smoothed out, and on the first occasion when the architect came to stay in the house, after it was finished and furnished and occupied, he said at breakfast: 'Well, if you must have pictures in a house I would as soon have your sort of pictures as any.' The house turned out a great success, and if it was a good deal more practical to live in as a result of Leslie Brooke's watchfulness over the architect's plans, it was beautifully proportioned and carried a particular distinction as a result of Clough's imagination and taste and flair. It was well built by an Oxford firm who knew their job, and welcomed the fact that they were building for an owner who was on the spot so that they were never kept waiting for answers or decisions.

The garden was Leslie Brooke's own creation. There was no one he had to defer to, apart from his wife who loved gardens too. He planned it and planted it and cherished it. Never before had he had such an opportunity, for the future garden was bare land, a corner cut off a large field which as recently as 1922 had produced a crop of wheat.

It speedily became apparent that first priority must be to create shelter from the prevailing south-west wind. An evergreen hedge had to be put in at once, and quick-growing trees and shrubs planted behind it. The site had so many assets; this wind, which whined round the house in a storm, was the sole liability.

The plan of the house included, of course, a studio, with admirable north light. But after the drawings for *Mad Shepherds* were finished, there ensued a period when Leslie Brooke spent more of his time poring over seed catalogues and shrub catalogues than working on pictures. He was determined that the garden should be lovely, and he studied books that would help him to fill it with unusual and beautiful varieties. The Cumnor garden was as truly one of his enduring creations as *Johnny Crow's Garden* was. Generously he conceded his son's request that there should be a hard tennis court, though its sandy colour was bound to clash with the green of the rest of the garden.

He found in the village an elderly man named Lock, retired from the Regular Army (where rumour had it he had served as a cook), who knew not much about gardening but was a steady digger, and at that early stage digging was wanted most. His method of coping with his employer's deafness, when he wished to draw his attention to anything, was to come up beside him and with his elbow give him a friendly nudge.

As a temporary assistant to help with the initial clearance of the land a seventeen-year-old boy from the village, Arthur Boyles, who happened to be looking for a job, was also taken on. Arthur became a friend to everyone. He soon ceased to be temporary. Indeed he worked in that garden for four successive owners, and when eventually he retired he had become the proud possessor of the medal awarded by the Royal Horticultural Society to a gardener who has been employed for more than fifty years continuously in the same garden.

It was November 1923 when the Brookes were at long last able to bring all their furniture out of store and move into the new house. When they had had to choose a name for it, they thought that they could not do better than consult old maps of the parish to see whether any special name had been attached to the corner of farmland which they had bought. This line of thought proved brighter in theory than in practice. They found the name, but it was Dung-croft.

So they had to make a fresh start. The idea occurred to them of perpetuating within the family the name of Uncle Somerset's house at Shere, which for nearly half a century had been a source of great happiness. After his death it had been sold to strangers. The name was Hurstcote.

Had there been less dear memories of it, they probably would not have made this name their first choice. But it also had local relev-ance. A mile or so out of the village, towards Oxford, was and is a small hill known as Cumnor Hurst. Matthew Arnold wrote of it in his fantasy poem *The Scholar Gypsy*—'Shepherds had met him on the Hurst in spring'—and again in *Thyrsis* he mentioned 'this rude Cumnor ground, its fir-topped Hurst, its farms, its quiet fields'.

Thus if they decided to call the new house Hurstcote, it would not be locally meaningless; and throughout the family it would be seen as a thread to link hoped-for happiness in the future with happiness of no ordinary measure in the past. So Hurstcote it be-came.

Cumnor, for all its proximity to Oxford, was still a village, and curiously under-equipped with public services. There was no mains water supply, no main drainage, no gas, no electricity, and a bus twice a week. The telephone number assigned to the Brookes was Cumnor 3. Out for a walk one day, Leslie Brooke got into talk over a gate with an elderly countryman at work in the fields, who said questioningly in a local Berkshire voice, 'Ye'll 'ave 'eerd of that there Oxford town?' This was spoken in 1923 within five miles of Oxford.

One by one the various public services arrived, and the gap between city and village was gradually closed by new building. Yet the village was not swallowed up by its great neighbour. It retained its own identity and life. Everyone knew everyone else, though newcomers like the Brookes were of course regarded as foreigners at first, till they became assimilated and accepted.

Over their choice of site and of architect they had no regrets. The design of the house with its studio and five bedrooms fulfilled all

Photograph taken in 1930 of Hurstcote,
the home and garden created by Leslie Brooke

their hopes. The planning and development of the garden lay as an exciting task ahead, which was going to demand plenty of imagination and hard work. They could start to repay the hospitality of their relatives and friends with whom they had been invited to stay during their two years of homelessness, all of whom unstintingly approved the new house. Experience showed how wise they had been in deciding to come to the neighbourhood of Oxford, where they had no lack of friends already.

The choice of Oxford also saved them from having to break all their links with London, and particularly with the world of art. Fast trains from Oxford made it simple to spend a day in London once or twice a month. They could visit their friends and relations there or arrange to meet them somewhere for lunch or tea, and there was seldom an art exhibition in London of interest to Leslie which he could not manage to see. He maintained his membership of the Savile Club, a society largely of artists and writers, and he seldom looked in there without meeting somebody he knew. He could call in on his publishers too when there was anything to discuss; and if ever he needed a new suit he could have it made for him by a London tailor, who was also a personal friend. 'Costly thy habit as thy purse will bear, but nought in fancy' was the Shakespearean precept which he used to quote. Intensely proud of the profession to which he belonged, in his dress he did not emphasise his membership of it. Throughout his married life he was accustomed to wear dark grey suits, with black shoes, a white shirt and a quiet tie, whether he was drawing or painting, reading or gardening. Often out of doors he would wear a cloth cap, especially in the garden.

As a joy, not as a chore, he dedicated himself to the conversion of an acre and a half of former cornfield into a garden. He planned its layout entirely himself, and of an evening he would concentrate on shrub catalogues, ever trying to find the out of the ordinary varieties rather than the common ones. He spent more time on choosing shrubs than seeds, because he was resolved to make a garden that would be labour-saving and not require an undue amount of looking after. This fitted in with his recognition that it was essential to plant hedges and shrubs and trees which as quickly as possible would produce windbreaks, to give shelter from the strong south-west gales.

He noted in diaries everything which he and Arthur put in from day to day, and he kept for purposes of garden record the invoices sent by the nurserymen from whom he used to order. A half-century later the 1923 prices came to look absurdly and enviably low.

In the course of time his policies for the garden proved to be amply justified. To avoid a windswept and empty look he put in more shrubs and trees than there would be room for as they grew larger, trusting that his eventual successors would realise that this had been deliberate policy and that the time would come when thinning out would be essential. But the original choice had been so well done that subsequent owners found it difficult to harden their hearts and remove beautiful growths whose only fault was that they had become overcrowded.

It was not until he was sixty-one that he first became a car owner. He never himself drove, but his wife as well as his son did, and he had Arthur taught. The principal difference that the car made to his way of life was that he no longer needed to depend on an inadequate bus service to take him to and from Oxford, unless he walked, which he did not mind doing. The car also eased the difficulty of keeping in touch with London, because he, and sometimes Sybil too, could be driven to Oxford station after breakfast and be met there in the evening, with seven hours in London to use as they liked. It is surprising how much one could accomplish in seven hours, helped by the comparative lightness of traffic in those days; and he was often able to reach his brother Henry's rooms in Hampstead for a cup of tea, before catching a six o'clock train back to Oxford.

At this stage in his life, while he was devoting a great part of his time to the planning and making of the Hurstcote garden, he had no further books in mind, but he accepted a number of commissions for bookplates and for portraits in black and red chalk. It made a difference that he had several friends among the Principals and Fellows of the women's Colleges, who frequently turned to him when the college wanted a drawing or a portrait for commemorative purposes. He had not the same personal contact with the men's Colleges, though some years later he was asked to do a black and red chalk drawing of the then Master of Balliol, A. D. Lindsay. Sandie Lindsay was a man of great distinction and left-wing views, so he had critics as well as admirers in the university. One of the severest critics, when he saw the drawing, said in all sincerity to the artist: 'I think you have got the Master at his very best.'

His slowly growing deafness became an advancing handicap to Leslie Brooke during his Cumnor years. He tried a number of hearing aids, but none much benefited him. He could still hear adequately if a person spoke straight to him and enunciated clearly, but in a general conversation he would not pick up enough to enable him to take part, and soft voices, if not raised, he could not hear at all. This led to situations which were often aggravating but sometimes comic. The Master's wife used to come while the drawing was in progress, and the artist welcomed this, because her presence and conversation would guard her husband's face from becoming fixed and set. But she spoke so softly that Leslie Brooke could seldom catch what she said. When an answer or comment from him was obviously expected, he had to direct his words to what he thought she had said, which sometimes bore the vaguest resemblance to what she had actually said. But she did not give up. Married as she was to a philosopher, and always seeking a meaning in everything, she took it for granted that there must have been some failure on her side, and that she was falling short and was not being intelligent.

Deafness did not seem to handicap him greatly in making contact with the Cumnor neighbours. They found him friendly, not withdrawn, and obviously ready to take his part in local activities. Saturday afternoons in summer would find him joining the spectators at the cricket field, a game he always enjoyed watching, whether or not his son was playing for the village that day. It was a pleasant though rough ground, and the ball was liable to be hit into a deterrent clump of nettles, if not into the muddy patch which originally had formed one of the fishponds. There was a small boy who used to earn sixpence for rescuing the ball from the fishpond; the talk was that he was always so grubby that it made little difference to him whether he had been into the mud or not.

In due course Sybil Brooke was encouraged by knowledgeable friends in Oxford to seek to get a Women's Institute established in

Chalk drawing of A. D. Lindsay,
Master of Balliol

Cumnor, for there was nothing outside the home to bring the women of the village together. It went well from the start; in those days there was no competition from television, and few people as yet had radio sets. She refused to be nominated President of the W.I., but agreed to become secretary. She was shy by nature, and in fact this was her first venture into any active form of public life. At the beginning it made her nervous even to have to read out the minutes of the last meeting, and the growing membership and evident enjoyment of the monthly meetings were her reward. But there was no satisfactory place for them to be held, and the Brookes played a part in furthering the idea of collecting money to build a village hall.

Meanwhile their thoughts were turning to the possibility of visiting Bergzabern a second time. The decision not to have the two graves moved to one of the Imperial War Graves Commission's cemeteries meant that the Commissioners' standard military headstones would not be available. So Leslie Brooke had designed two headstones to be made in London of Hoptonwood stone and shipped to Bergzabern, where the burgomaster was willing to have them erected. By the beginning of 1925 this had been done, and the main object of a second visit there was to see how the graves were being cared for and how the new headstones looked.

They went in April, and came away well satisfied. Everything had been done exactly as they wished. The original wooden crosses with their simple metal plates had been kept for them when the headstones were erected, and these they brought back to England. The one they sent to the Provans in Glasgow; the other was kept and treasured by Sybil Brooke where it hung on the wall of her room for the rest of her life.

Leonard's parents did not expect they would ever be at Bergzabern again. In the cemetery they had taken new photographs of the graves with the headstones in place, and they had the wooden cross as a further reminder. In fact, Henry and his wife Barbara, whom he married in 1933, were the next members of the family to visit Bergzabern, which they did in 1938, and were able to send back a full description and fresh photographs, just twelve months before the Second World War broke out.

In that war, Bergzabern did not escape untouched. The small town came under shell fire. Damage was done in the cemetery, and the British headstones were broken, as were those of many of the German graves. Furthermore, there were a number of fresh British graves, and when this war was over the Imperial War Graves Commission wrote that they would now accept responsibility for all the British who were buried in the Bergzabern cemetery, including the provision of the standard British military headstones. By this time Leslie Brooke had died, but Leonard's mother and brother felt all the more satisfied that the decision not to ask for his grave to be moved elsewhere had been the right one. They found that they were left with nothing but friendly feelings towards the little town of Bergzabern.

When they returned to England, a fresh anxiety fell upon them. It had become obvious that Leslie's much-loved brother Henry, who was now sixty-four, had been lastingly pulled down by his overwork following the fire at Trent in 1922. Eventually the doctors insisted that he must endure an exploratory operation. At first he seemed to have come through that successfully, but he was slow to regain any strength, and on 3 August 1925 in a London nursing home he died peacefully.

To Sybil he had always been more like a brother than a brother-in-law. To his nephews he had been a devoted uncle. His sister Rhoda and her husband, now Sir Graham Balfour, loved him dearly. He was a man of pure selflessness. The bonds of affection between the Brookes and the Balfours were as close as could be, and now there would be no more of the blissful holidays in Normandy which the three men had been accustomed to take together. He was buried beside his parents in Flaybrick Hill cemetery, Birkenhead, near their childhood home where Henry and Leslie and Rhoda had grown up together.

The Balfours had long planned to return and take a house in Oxford, when Graham's distinguished period of service as Director of Education for Staffordshire came to an end. They chose for their retirement a small house in Blackhall Road, a quiet spot close to the centre of Oxford, untroubled by the noise and dust of traffic. This meant that the Oxford neighbourhood was now the home of Leslie's sister as well as two of Sybil's sisters, Olive Jacks and Maud Rolleston; and all four families knew each other well and saw a good deal of one another.

Visits to London, however, did not become less frequent. Several were needed, of course, for clearing up Brother Henry's affairs and disposal of his possessions. All in all, there was plenty of work to be done, in addition to pursuing the completion of the Hurstcote garden; and this explained the long interval before Leslie set to work on children's books again.

He wanted to try his hand at producing a third Johnny Crow, but twenty years had passed since the second, and he was reticent and unsure of his ability, after so long a gap, to recover his Johnny Crow touch and to attain the former standard. There would be no trouble about material; he had kept a note of many rhymes, with animals attached, which had been devised at the time of the earlier books but never, in fact, been used, and the list had been augmented occasionally in the twenty years when bright ideas had crossed his mind and been rescued from oblivion. By the spring of 1928 he was starting to try his hand at rough sketches for pictures which might one day crystallise into finished drawings for a third instalment.

Jacob Toad explains to his wife why
he wonders if the world is round,
from *A Roundabout Turn*

X   Jacob Toad

Then in August 1928 his thoughts were diverted. For many years the family had been taking the weekly magazine *Punch*, and turning over its pages one day he happened on a poem which he thought he would like to illustrate. It was called *A Roundabout Turn*, and concerned the adventures of a toad who wanted to find out whether the world was really round, as it was alleged to be.

The editor kindly put him in touch with the author, who turned out to be Mr Robert Charles, a civil servant, one of His Majesty's Inspectors of Education. He was pleased and co-operative. He had been spending a family holiday near Shere and Albury, and when a travelling fair had set up on Albury Heath one summer day, and a toad was spotted making its laborious way in the direction of the fair, Robert Charles had made up the story and the verses for the amusement of his wife and children, who said that he ought to send them to *Punch*.

Warne, the publishers, had been asking Leslie Brooke for some time when he was going to do another children's book for them, and they welcomed this idea, and terms were arranged, *Punch* giving their permission. It was some years later that Mr Charles was promoted to be Chief Inspector of Schools and appointed a C.B.E. Those whose books Leslie Brooke illustrated had a habit of subsequently appearing in the twice-yearly Honours List, not through any causal connection but to reward their merits in other directions.

The first practical step for the artist was to find a toad, for toads, unlike pigs and bears, were not a normal part of his animal repertoire. Fortunately the Hurstcote garden produced a fine specimen who for the duration of the drawings became almost one of the family. To enable him to be recognised again if need be, Leslie dropped a tiny spot of paint on his forehead. He also made inquiries of a keeper at the London Zoo about the habits and diets of toads, and learnt incidentally that the approved way of picking up a toad was to pinch between forefinger and thumb the loose skin on its back.

Mr and Mrs Toad appear to have lived in a small house where she remained when her husband went out to discover whether or not the world was round. Framed on the wall of their sitting-room

'It's a long way down the road
For a fellow that walks as slow as a
Toad'

was the motto 'Hop On, Hop Ever', and on the side table stood a photograph of one of their children, a tadpole. She had just started knitting a long stocking for her husband at the hour when he went out, and the passing of time was indicated in subsequent pictures by the growth of her knitting, until he returned in the evening. He was reading a newspaper called *The Weekly Croak* when he first heard the sound of the fair arriving. He must have taken some time to reach it, because, as he truly observed, 'It's a long way down the road for a fellow that walks as slow as a Toad.' The road in that picture is the one which runs south across Albury Heath, towards Farley Green. On the horizon one could just spot the arms of a windmill, a landmark which is still there but is nowadays hidden by the growth of surrounding trees. The Silent Pool, title of a picture on the wall of the toad's sitting-room, is the name of a beauty-spot not far from Albury Heath, doubtless the home of many toads.

The drawing of the toad about to be picked up by the small girl and put on the roundabout is another of the few pictures in any of the Leslie Brooke children's books which depict a person in what at the time (1930) was modern dress, for whenever he could he avoided drawing humans whose clothes would cause pictures to date.

Jacob Toad, as the hero of the verse signs himself, was released from the studio to the garden as soon as his part was done. He seemed to bear no malice, for he was often seen again, and identified by the spot of red paint, after his foray into literature was over.

A Roundabout Turn was printed and published in time for Christmas 1930, and was particularly successful. This was partly due to the growing American interest in Leslie Brooke's work among children's librarians there, stimulated by the keen enthusiasm shown by the head of the Children's Department of the New York Public Library, Miss Anne Carroll Moore.

They had originally met in his St John's Wood studio in 1921 shortly before the Brookes left London, and they had developed a friendship by correspondence which lasted for the rest of his life. She kept him in touch with what was happening in the world of American children's books, and he would answer her questions about his work and that of other English illustrators. She introduced to him

The Horn Book, the magazine of children's books published in Boston, Massachusetts. In the Cumnor days she would give any American illustrator planning to spend a holiday in England an introduction to Leslie Brooke, and they would often bring with them a copy of their latest book to leave with him as a keepsake, with the result that he built up a representative collection of contemporary American children's literature, much appreciated by him and his wife and later on by his grandchildren. His American connection spread of course to Miss Moore's friends and fellow librarians, and brought a very real new interest into his life.

One of them told of an incident which moved his heart. She had been reading aloud *The Three Bears* to a group of Harlem children, when a small black girl suddenly exclaimed, 'To think they each had a bed! And they only bears.'

Not long after the publication of *A Roundabout Turn*, he received a letter from a Mrs King of North Carolina which in charming terms inquired whether he could bring himself to design a bookplate for her daughter Virginia's seventh birthday. The letter touched him and started a correspondence which led to the production of a bookplate wherein Brer Rabbit as drawn by A. B. Frost in *Uncle Remus* and the White Rabbit as drawn by John Tenniel in *Alice's Adventures in Wonderland* meet together in a briar patch, with Johnny Crow looking down from a tree in the background. As he explained to Mrs King, the artist was going to have to solve two practical problems: first, how to blend successfully the differing styles of Frost and Tenniel with his own, and secondly how to design a bookplate which Virginia would enjoy at the age of seven without wishing to discard it as childish when she was seventeen. Happily the bookplate proved to be a great success.

Leslie Brooke was sixty-eight when he completed the drawings of *A Roundabout Turn*. The house at Cumnor was seven years old, and the making of the garden out of a cornfield was mainly finished, though there would always be plenty of work to do in keeping it up. When they took the decision to build at Cumnor, they looked on it as their retirement home, and all their planning and planting had been with this in view.

However, doubts began sadly to arise. The labour entailed in

A bookplate for
Virginia King's seventh birthday

maintaining the garden was one factor, not an immediate one, but a consideration which would need to be borne in mind as Leslie grew older and his powers to take his share in the work of the garden would, in the nature of things, begin to ebb. Much more serious, however, were the growing signs that climatically it was not the place for Sybil. Even with all the planting of hedges and shrubs for shelter that had been done, the prevailing south-west winds blowing from the Berkshire downs across the Vale of the White Horse afflicted her, stirring up the neuralgic pains from which she suffered, on and off, throughout her life. This was aggravated, the doctors said, by her husband's gradually worsening deafness, which obliged her to raise her voice whenever she was talking with him; yet even so he might miss part of what was said. Constant effort to make oneself heard is not the best accompaniment of nerve pain.

From 1930 onwards the Brookes had this problem to wrestle with. They might have stayed on for several more years than they did, but what clinched their decision to leave was that in 1932 their son Henry became engaged to be married to a red-haired girl named Barbara, daughter of Canon A. A. Mathews, who was vicar of a largely working-class parish in Newport, Monmouthshire. She had spent three years at a domestic science training college in Gloucester, followed by two years teaching domestic science at a school in Dagenham under the Essex County Council. Realisation came to her by then that she did not really want to spend the rest of her life teaching in schools, and would prefer to earn her living as a nurse than as a teacher, so she changed her job and entered the Nightingale Training School as a probationer. She loved this, though by getting engaged to Henry Brooke at the end of a year she became, in official terms, wastage to the nursing profession.

He was at that time working for the Conservative Research Department, and it was obvious that they would be setting up house in or near London. They were against the idea of commuting, and eventually settled in Hampstead, close to the Heath.

By that time Leslie and Sybil had virtually decided that for her health they could not stay on at Cumnor indefinitely, and their one way of continuing to see much of their son and daughter-in-law, not to speak of any future grandchildren, would be by selling Hurstcote and following them to London.

So things turned out. It was a grievous blow to Leslie, though typically he never allowed anyone outside his immediate family to see it. The garden on which for ten years he had lavished love, time and care would cease to be his, and the maturing of all that he had put into it, in thought as well as work, would be for others to enjoy.

XI   *Johnny Crow's New Garden*

Leslie Brooke started on the pictures for another book before he left Cumnor. For long he had had at the back of his mind—right at the back—the possibility of producing a third Johnny Crow book.

The question for him was whether his gifts of art and humour would have fallen away, after the long interval of twenty-five years. The first sequel to *Johnny Crow's Garden* had succeeded, and was still selling well. But could he do a second sequel that would be up to standard? Could he take the risk of failure?

His wife, once again, strongly encouraged him. He believed that he should be able to bring it off, but realised what he was hazarding. Sybil, with the practical good sense that characterised her, argued that he could only find out the answer if he tried. So the 1907 lists were dug out, and the title *Johnny Crow's New Garden* was easily settled on.

There never was a real garden, any more than there was a real Johnny Crow. Nothing in the two earlier books had been copied from, or bore any perceptible relation to, the garden at Harwell where the Brookes were living at the time. Likewise the garden at Cumnor, though in every sense a new garden, was not a basis nor an inspiration for any of the pictures in the third book. It was only in later years that a slow-growing yew in the Cumnor garden reached a height at which it became feasible to model Johnny Crow in topiary.

Johnny Crow's New Garden, which was completed and published in 1935, was dedicated to the first grandchild, Peter, who had been born in London in March 1934, just before Hurstcote was vacated. No one looking at the three books together could have deduced from the nature or quality of the pictures that whereas the 'Garden' and the 'Party' were done at the age of forty and forty-four respectively, the 'New Garden' was the work of a man of seventy-two. The magic was still there. The secret was that in his mind and his art Leslie Brooke remained as close to the child's outlook as ever he had been.

Part of the skill was to design the pictures so that the child, if he looked carefully enough, would find in them the answers to the many questions he might ask. The Deer came over very queer because he had rashly been nibbling the laburnum; there is no mention of that in the letterpress, but the background in a previous drawing has disclosed it. The Bear with the help of the Chimpanzees changed into his day-time clothes so that the loan of his slumberwear could help in the process of getting the Deer better by degrees; this is inferred but not stated.

The Donkey was walking between the trees when he overheard the Cow singing duets with the Sow. They had dropped on the ground in front of them the score of *The Farmer's Boy*, in the appropriate key of B sharp. The Baboon, a music critic whose habit was to preface any remark with the word 'Yes', doubtless understated the truth when he pronounced the Donkey to be sadly out of tune.

One of the rare ambiguities in the Leslie Brooke books was the identity of John, who was at risk of catching the weasel's measles. Some have supposed it to refer to Johnny Crow himself, but this was not so. John was the fluffy cygnet whom the two swans in the frontispiece were ready to defend against all comers, including germs. In the picture of all the animals expressing their gratitude, Johnny Crow can be seen having a word with them. Naturally every animal can be found there, if one looks.

The Lion had been the first to arrive in 1903, and was the last to leave in 1935. To show that it was all over, he had taken off his green and yellow tie and draped it between two upright evergreens, and was saying good-bye with an almost human expression to Johnny Crow, who was modestly confident of having been a successful host once more.

The Deer in borrowed slumberwear, lent by the Bear

The choral efforts of the Trio inspired
the pheasant to say: 'It's most unpleasant'

'Yes,' said
   the Baboon,
'He is sadly
   out of tune'

The Lion gives his
green and yellow tie
to his host as a
gesture of
Royal gratitude

There was never any question of a fourth Johnny Crow book. But there were many animals and rhymes left on record which for one reason or another had been unused or crowded out. One possibility, never seriously favoured, had been a change of scene.

Johnny Crow
Was feeling low
And required a little holiday.
For the Bantam
Said: 'You're looking quite a phantom.'
'Well', said the Guinea Fowl,
'You're a pretty skinny fowl.'
And the Tits
Said: 'Try Biarritz',
But the Geese
Said: 'No place like Nice,'
For Johnny Crow's holiday.

And the Yak
Helped to pack.
But the Puffin
Said: 'You'll never get enough in,'
And the Ox
Sat on the box.

And the Yak
Welcomed him back,
And the Gazelle
Said: 'You're looking very well.'
And the Cow
Said: 'We're very happy now
In Johnny Crow's Garden.'

This was the only long piece of connected description. The remainder consisted of the names of animals with possible rhymes for them. Some were discarded because, however apt otherwise, they would not lend themselves to illustration.

Then the Baboon
Drew attention to the Moon,
And the Chameleon
Said: 'It's near its perihelion,'
And the Tench
Said: 'Don't talk French.'

And the Gnu
Cooked a dish of Irish stew,
And the Leveret
Said: 'That's the best I ever ate,'
But the Bustard
Took too much mustard.

Then the Macaw
Said: 'Let's explore.'
But the Toucan
Said: 'I won't—You can.'

And the Gorilla
Was allowed to build a villa,
And the Lynx
Peeped through the chinks,
And the Terrier
Said: 'The more the merrier.'

Then the Turtle
Was decked out with myrtle,
And the Cougar
Took porridge with sugar,
But the Cheetah
Liked it even sweeter.
As for the Leopard,
He preferred his peppered,
And the Puffin
Couldn't put enough in.

Then the Crab
Said: 'Fetch me a cab,'
But the Lobster
Wouldn't from the hob stir,
And the Squid
Said: 'Well, I never did.'

And the Newt
Was inclined to dispute,
And the Spider
Said: 'Try a mug of cider,'
And the Beetle
Said: 'Just a leetle,'
And the Pig
Said: 'I'm merry as a grig.'
But the Duck
Was so fat that she stuck.

Finally we have those two somewhat mysterious birds, the penguins, who stalk in and out of the pictures. It may be held that they earn no marks at all. But perhaps for that very reason they deserve a mention here. At any rate they are never out of step.

And the Penguins
Didn't do anything
(Didn't even rhyme)
In Johnny Crow's Garden.

The expressions on the faces of animals which he was constantly drawing, such as bears and pigs, came straight out of his own head. Also, for most of his working life, he was within reach of the London Zoo, where he could study and sketch wild animals in their cages, if he had any doubts about the set of their heads or the ripple of their muscles. There was also the Natural History Museum in South Kensington, where he could find almost anything from skeletons of dinosaurs and pterodactyls to stuffed hedgehogs rolled up into prickly balls.

   In addition he kept and used all his life as his constant standby a large book entitled *All about Animals*, consisting of some 240 superb photographs published about 1895 by George Newnes in collaboration with the Zoological Society. He did not copy from these or other photographs, but used them as a check or a reminder when he had to draw an animal which was not familiar to him. What he would never do was to fudge or blur a drawing so as to conceal any uncertainty existing in his own mind. Because he had had no previous occasion to draw a llama or a tapir, for example, he paid a special visit to the Natural History Museum to study their shapes and the pattern of their muscles.

"GOOD-BYE!"

XII   Drawing to the End

Leslie Brooke's 70th birthday was the last but one he spent at Cumnor, and he was overjoyed to receive in celebration of it a scroll from his friends across the Atlantic. Unrolled, it consisted of messages from heads of children's departments in public libraries and sketches by living American illustrators of children's books who wished to join in congratulations to him. This touched him deeply, and there was no doubt of their desire to do him honour. They had been among the first to acknowledge the contribution that his work had made towards raising the standard of American illustrations for children's books, which with few exceptions had been relatively undistinguished up to the turn of the century.

His drawings for the 'New Garden' had been started at Cumnor but finished at his new home in Hampstead, and the book was published in 1935, on his seventy-third birthday. It received a warm welcome in the book trade and in children's libraries on both sides of the Atlantic, though not becoming as well known as its two more famous predecessors. This was not due to any shortfall in quality, because technically it contains some of his best animal work.

On selling Hurstcote and returning to London, Sybil and Leslie Brooke moved to a house with a small front and back garden, some ten minutes walk from the house of their son and daughter-in-law and first grandchild. A front room on the first floor could be made into a studio, having two large windows that faced north-east. It was not perfect for its purpose, but it would pass muster. He frankly recognised that his professional work was drawing to its close, though he would still receive commissions for black and red chalk portraits and the like. He drew Peter in 1938, but did not have opportunity to do the same for his second grandson, another Henry, born in July 1936, for it was a principle with him not to draw a child until he was past his third birthday, because it seemed to him cruel to make a child under that age sit still for long enough.

Both grandsons were a source of immense pleasure to him, and this was one of the recompenses for losing Cumnor. An even greater one was his wife's health. Unquestionably she was the better for the move; her neuralgic pain was markedly lessened, now that she was no longer at the mercy of strong winds blowing over miles of open countryside.

There was another and decisive counterweight which did not come into the reckoning in 1933 when the decision to move was taken, but which grew and grew with the years. This was the prospect of war. The upkeep of Hurstcote, house and garden, under war conditions would have grown inexorably harder, had 1939 found them still living there, with Leslie aged seventy-six and Sybil sixty-nine.

Arthur would doubtless have been classed as being in a reserved occupation, and therefore disqualified for military service, provided that he devoted all his time to the vegetable garden; but his employer could not possibly have managed the flower garden single-handed, and as he approached the age of eighty would have been able to do less and less in it, however willing the spirit was. Petrol rationing would have drastically curtailed their ability to reach Oxford and the power of their friends to visit them, and wartime frustrations and shortages would not have left them unscathed. It would have been a troubled household, out of easy reach of help. Far better was it that they should have moved to London and a less isolated life, with fewer individual responsibilities and problems, even though there might be greater exposure to air raids. But all this could hardly have been measured up and taken into the reckoning, at the time of moving in 1934. Hypothetical possibilities could not at that time have mitigated the loss of the garden.

Leslie also missed his daily walk along country lanes, which had been such a happy feature of life at Cumnor. For years he had relied on walking for exercise and pleasure. He had not been able to afford expensive holidays or recreations when he was younger. That never irked him, for he enjoyed walking, wherever he was, and would not have willingly changed his chosen way of life. It was sad for him

125

A photograph of Sybil and Leslie Brooke in 1936,
in the garden doorway of their last home in Hampstead

that Sybil, following Leonard's birth, had been warned by doctors not to overtax her strength by taking long walks; otherwise she would gladly have accompanied him. Their home from 1934 on was fortunately within a few hundred yards of Hampstead Heath, which was the next best thing to fields and the country.

As he grew older he read more and more—memoirs and historical books, not novels. Had television been available, he would have revelled in it. He had acquired his first radio, then commonly called wireless, when he was about sixty-four, and it brought music back into his life, from which deafness had long excluded him. But he was disappointed with a succession of hearing aids that he tried; he never managed to hear as fully or clearly as he hoped.

He never lost his enthusiasm for art, and never, so to speak, laid down his pencil or paint-brush. In the last year of his life he was actually planning a new children's book. This was to be a collaborative venture between him and Sybil. Years ago she had written a short story for children about Mr Nobody, who lived up to his name and had no body, and longed to be like other people and have a body. There was a goose in the tale, and also a pig, two creatures which he relished drawing. He had completed six of the black-and-white drawings for *Mr Nobody* and was still working on the book, when he fell ill. His hand kept up its gaiety to the end.

One of the features of his career as a children's artist was that his workmanship and his humour never flagged. It was by the friendliness and the kindliness which shone through all his drawings that he first captured the minds of children and then held them for over fifty years; and there was no falling away, as age crept on him. He paid children the compliment of putting into their hands pictures which of themselves tell almost the whole story; pictures which gave children the answers to their natural questions, if they will look carefully enough to frame their questions, and then turn over the pages to find the answers. The doings of the animals may be absurdities, but they are essentially reasonable and understandable absurdities; and they were never frightening or horrific. The expressions on the faces of pigs or bears are the fruit of lifelong sympathetic observation; one has never caught quite that emotion on the face of a real pig, but it would come as no surprise if one did.

127

'Mr Nobody', one of the six
finished drawings for a story on
which Leslie Brooke was working
when he died

Despite the growing threat of war, it was granted to Leslie Brooke to live his remaining years quietly. He was back among his London friends. From time to time he received visits from his fellow-craftsmen and admirers in North America. He was close enough to his son and daughter-in-law and grandsons to see them constantly and to enter into their lives. His wife was always at his side; and it gave pleasure to them both when in 1938 their son Henry was elected to Parliament.

At the outbreak of war in September 1939, elderly people in London and the big cities which were considered specially vulnerable were urged to make their own arrangements to leave home and go to safer places if they could. Leslie's sister, Lady Balfour, whose husband had died in 1929, urged them to come and join her in her Oxford home. So they shut up their Hampstead house and accepted her invitation, no one knowing what to expect, no one making plans far ahead. There ensued seven months of what came to be called 'the phoney war'. As nothing happened to London, and thousands of children were drifting home from the reception areas to which they and their schools had been hastily evacuated, Leslie and Sybil decided to return too, and found their home intact as they had left it.

They did not move again during his lifetime. As winter turned to spring Leslie, who had passed his seventy-seventh birthday at Oxford, fell ill, and on 1 May 1940 he peacefully died at home. He was spared the hazards of war, for up to that date hardly one bomb had fallen on British soil.

It had long been a joke in the Brooke family that, if he should come to die in Hampstead, the undertakers he would like employed would be the Hampstead firm of J. Crowe and Sons. And so it was. The joke was not disclosed to them, but it was thoroughly enjoyed by the whole Brooke family.

Like most young art students Leslie Brooke set out on his chosen profession with the ambition and the hope to become a great artist, to earn the initials R.A., to rise to the top, and to make a name for himself in the history of art. Man proposes, God disposes. In the form which it took originally, that ambition was unfulfilled. But in the end would Leslie Brooke have wished it otherwise? In a tribute to him in the *Horn Book* of May, 1941, the librarian of a New York City Branch Library with a sense of humour wrote: 'How wonderful to have created those books! I've been studying *Hamlet*. But I don't know; it has its points, to be sure, but oh, to have given such rapture to children. Yes, I think I'd rather be Brooke than Shakespeare!'

Many years later, a member of the Brooke family received in a letter from a friend perhaps the most penetrating tribute ever paid to Johnny Crow, and implicitly to his author. 'We were much fascinated about Johnny Crow, who is one of our favourite characters, one of the best of all books on Pastoral Care, comparable to the learned treatise on the subject by Pope Gregory the Great.' The writer was Professor of Ecclesiastical History in the University of Cambridge, so he ought to know.

Acknowledgments

The author would like to give his warm thanks to Grace Hogarth for her invaluable advice, assistance and encouragement throughout the work on this book, and also to Valerie and Brian Alderson for compiling the check-list which appears on pages 133–139. The illustration on page 27 from *A Spring Song* by T. Nash is reproduced by kind permission of J. M. Dent & Sons Ltd; those on pages 34, 35, and 36 from *Travels Round our Village* by Miss E. G. Hayden are reproduced by kind permission of Constable & Company Ltd; the illustration 'Civilisation' on page 37 appears by kind permission of *Punch;* and the illustration of Snarley Bob from *Mad Shepherds* by L. P. Jacks, by kind permission of Ernest Benn Ltd.

132

Leslie Brooke's
Book Illustrations: A Check-list

Compiled by
Brian and Valerie Alderson

We have attempted here to give a full list of all the books illustrated by Leslie Brooke in chronological order. Along with standard information drawn from the title-pages, we have included notes on the number of drawings or decorations made by the artist, their manner of reproduction, and the appearance of original work on bindings. Most of the line and half-tone illustrations will have been transferred photographically to blocks or plates from the artist's original drawings or water-colours.

Abbreviations used are: pp. for pages; front. for frontispiece; t.p. for title-page. The term 'inset' has been used to indicate the inclusion of leaves additional to those given in the pagination.

1   EVELYN EVERETT-GREEN. *Miriam's Ambition; a story for children*. Blackie, [1889]
    $7'' \times 4\frac{1}{2}''$. 224 pp. (+ 32 pp. adverts). Inset front. and 3 plates, line. Probably published simultaneously with the following item, although that is dated 1890.
2   MARY C. ROWSELL. *Thorndyke Manor; a tale of Jacobite times*. Blackie, 1890 [published 1889]
    $7\frac{3}{8}'' \times 4\frac{1}{2}''$. 288 pp. (+ 32 pp. adverts). Inset front. and 5 plates, line.
    Binding: Decorated brown cloth with a drawing by LLB blocked on front in black and gilt.
3   EVELYN EVERETT-GREEN. *The Secret of the Old House; a story for children*. Blackie, [1890]
    $7\frac{3}{8}'' \times 4\frac{3}{4}''$. 224 pp. Inset front. and 3 plates, line.
4   GEORGE MACDONALD. *The Light Princess, and Other Fairy Stories* [i.e. 'The Giant's Heart' and 'The Golden Key'] Blackie, [1890]
    $7'' \times 4\frac{1}{2}''$. 192 pp. (+ 16 pp. adverts). Inset front. and 2 plates, line.

5   MARY L. MOLESWORTH. *Nurse Heatherdale's Story*. Macmillan, 1891
$7\frac{1}{4}'' \times 4\frac{1}{2}''$. 202 pp. Picture t.p. + inset front. and 6 plates, line.
Binding: Red cloth with floral decoration on front and spine in black by LLB.

6   ANNIE E. ARMSTRONG. *Marian; or, the Abbey Grange*. Blackie, 1892
$7'' \times 4\frac{1}{2}''$. 224 pp. (+32 pp. adverts). Inset front. and 3 plates, unusually in monochrome half-tone, reproduced from wash drawings.

7   L. T. MEADE. *A Ring of Rubies*. A. D. Innes & Co., 1892
$7\frac{1}{8}'' \times 4\frac{5}{8}''$. 320 pp. (+6 pp. adverts.). Inset front. and 3 plates, line.

8   MARY L. MOLESWORTH. *The Girls and I; a veracious history*. Macmillan, 1892
As 5 above, but with 200 pp.

9   ISMAY THORN. *Bab, or the triumph of unselfishness*. Blackie, 1892.
$7'' \times 4\frac{1}{2}''$. 192 pp. (+32 pp. adverts). Inset front. and 2 plates, half-tone wash.

10   ROMA WHITE (Blanche Oram). *Brownies and Rose-leaves*. A. D. Innes & Co., 1892 (The Rose-leaf Library)
$7\frac{3}{4}'' \times 5''$. 200 pp. including front. and 6 plates, with ten drawings in text by LLB. There are also two plates showing beefy elves 'designed and drawn by S. Schofield'.
Binding: Beige cloth with decorations on front and spine by LLB. Parts of these later figured as illustrations in 15 below.

11   EVA KNATCHBULL HUGESSEN. *A Hit and a Miss*. A. D. Innes & Co., 1893 (The Dainty Books)
$5\frac{3}{4}'' \times 5''$. 155 pp. (+4 pp. adverts) including front. and 4 full-page and 6 smaller illustrations in the text, line.

12   MARY L. MOLESWORTH. *Mary; a nursery story for very little children*. Macmillan, 1893
As 5 above, but with 190 pp. (+4 pp. adverts).

13   AMY WALTON. *Penelope and the Others; a story of five country children*. Blackie, 1893 [published 1892]
$7'' \times 4\frac{1}{2}''$. 224 pp. (+32 pp. adverts). Inset front. and 3 plates, half-tone wash.

14   MARY L. MOLESWORTH. *My New Home*. Macmillan, 1894.
As 5 above, but with 208 pp. and a pictorial decoration on the binding.

15   ROMA WHITE. *Moonbeams and Brownies*. A. D. Innes & Co., 1894 (The Dainty Books)
$5\frac{3}{4}'' \times 5''$. 160 pp. including front. and 6 full-page and 6 smaller illus-

trations in the text, line. Two unusual illustrations on pp. 38 and 94 appear to have been made from decorations prepared for use on bindings and may have been inserted by the publisher. They are not signed.

16   MARY L. MOLESWORTH. *The Carved Lions*. Macmillan, 1895
As 5 above, but with 206 pp. and a binding of blue cloth with leonine devices by LLB.

17   MARY L. MOLESWORTH. *Sheila's Mystery*. Macmillan, 1895
As 5 above, but with 210 pp. and a binding of blue cloth with a pictorial design by LLB.

18   MARY L. MOLESWORTH. *The Oriel Window*. Macmillan, 1896
As 5 above, but with 194 pp. and a pictorial design on the binding.

19   E. H. STRAIN. *School in Fairyland*. T. Fisher Unwin, 1896
$7\frac{1}{2}'' \times 4\frac{7}{8}''$. 186 pp. ($+6$ pp. adverts etc.). Inset front. and 6 plates, line.
Binding: Green cloth with the illustration facing p. 64 stamped on front.

20   ANDREW LANG ed. *The Nursery Rhyme Book*. Warne, 1897
$7\frac{3}{4}'' \times 5\frac{3}{8}''$. 288 pp. decorative t.p., 107 illustrations and decorative end-papers, line.
In 1916 an edition entitled *Nursery Rhymes* was published by Warne in smaller format ($6\frac{1}{2}'' \times 4\frac{1}{2}''$), with 140 pp. It had a pictorial t.p. and 61 line drawings in the text plus 24 drawings converted into inset colour plates in half-tone, letterpress. It had a fawn dust-wrapper incorporating a plate of Humpty-Dumpty taken from the book. This bound volume was itself split into three individual booklets in the same year: *Rhymes and Lullabies*, *Song and Ditties*, and *Tales and Jingles* [not seen].
In compiling this collection LLB worked from a large-paper copy of James Orchard Halliwell's *The Nursery Rhymes of England* published by Warne in 1886.

21   MARY L. MOLESWORTH. *Miss Mouse and her Boys*. Macmillan, 1897
As above, but with 210 pp. and a pictorial design on the binding.

22   ROBERT BROWNING. *Pippa Passes; a drama*. Duckworth, 1898
$8\frac{3}{4}'' \times 6\frac{3}{4}''$. 72 pp. Inset front. and 6 plates, engraved by Lemercier and printed in Paris. The book was printed on Japanese vellum in an edition limited to 60 copies. A less imposing trade edition ($7\frac{7}{8}'' \times 6\frac{1}{2}''$), bound in dark green cloth, was issued on paper.

23   T[homas] NASH. *A Spring Song, now again published*...J. M. Dent & Co., 1898
$6\frac{7}{8}'' \times 4\frac{1}{2}''$. 16 folios, each including a colour picture or decoration

'engraved and printed [from wood] by Edmund Evans'.

24   ARTHUR SOMERVELL. *Singing Time; a child's song-book.* Archibald Constable & Co., 1899
$11\frac{1}{8}'' \times 8\frac{3}{4}''$. 48 pp. with front., decorative dedication and 12 line drawings in text. All the lettering of the songs is by LLB.
Binding: Decorative boards with an illustration $7\frac{1}{2}'' \times 7\frac{1}{2}''$ on front and back in olive and gold.

25   EDWARD LEAR. *The Pelican Chorus, and Other Verses.* Warne [1899?]
$8\frac{1}{2}'' \times 6\frac{5}{8}''$. 64 pp. Inset front., decorative t.p. and 6 plates in half-tone litho. 30 line illustrations in text.
Binding: Decorated paper boards in colour by LLB (unsigned) with decorative endpapers in line. A later edition was quarter cloth with red paper boards blind-stamped, lettered in white and with a half-tone colour plate (not in the book) laid on ($5\frac{1}{8}'' \times 4\frac{3}{4}''$). LLB's own copy of this book was given to his wife in December 1899. The BM copy arrived in March 1900.

26   EDWARD LEAR. *The Jumblies and Other Nonsense Verses.* Warne, [November, 1900]
As previous item, but with 32 line illustrations in the text, and a later alternative binding with grey/blue paper boards.
These two titles were also issued in one volume, as *Nonsense Songs*, in November, 1900. The binding was brown cloth blind-stamped on the front with an enlarged version of LLB's drawing of the owl with a guitar. LLB compiled these two volumes from a copy of the *Nonsense Songs and Stories* published by Warne in 1897.

27   ELEANOR G. HAYDEN. *Travels Round our Village.* Archibald Constable & Co., 1901
$8\frac{3}{4}'' \times 5\frac{1}{2}''$. 322 pp. (+14 pp. adverts) including front. and 7 full-page and 26 other illustrations, line.

28   L. LESLIE BROOKE. *Johnny Crow's Garden; a picture book.* Warne, 1903
$8\frac{1}{8}'' \times 6\frac{1}{4}''$. 48 pp. including decorated t.p., half-title vignette, hand-lettered dedication and 36 line drawings + inset front. and 7 plates in half-tone litho. Decorated end-papers.
Binding: Quarter cloth, red paper boards with oblong half-tone on front ($3\frac{5}{8}'' \times 2\frac{3}{8}''$).

29   ANTHONY TROLLOPE. *Barchester Towers.* Blackie, 1903
$7\frac{3}{4}'' \times 5''$. 426 pp. Inset front. and 5 plates, line.

30   *The Story of the Three Little Pigs.* Warne, [1904]
$10'' \times 8''$. 24 pp. including pictorial t.p., 8 full-page plates in half-tone litho and 15 line drawings in text.

Binding: Wrap-round card with colour designs on outer face and monochrome on inner by LLB.

31   *Tom Thumb*. Warne, [1904]

As previous item but with 16 line drawings in text.

These two titles were issued as the first series of *Leslie Brooke's Children's Books* in one volume for Christmas, 1904, bound in beige cloth with a decoration in pink and green by LLB.

32   *The Golden Goose*. Warne, [1905]

As 30 above, but with 14 line drawings in text.

33   *The Three Bears*. Warne, [1905]

As previous item.

These two titles formed the second series of *Leslie Brooke's Children's Books* and were issued as such in one volume in 1905, while at the same date the four titles of the two series appeared in the one-volume *Golden Goose Book*, bound in light green cloth with a decoration on the front in red and gilt by LLB.

34   EMILY LAWLESS. *The Book of Gilly; four months out of a life.* Smith, Elder & Co., 1906

8″ × 6″. 298 pp. (+ 2 pp advert). Inset front. and 3 plates, half-tone chalk.

In 1902 Isbister had published Lawless's verses *With the Wild Geese* with an introduction by Stopford A. Brooke.

35   L. LESLIE BROOKE. *Johnny Crow's Party; another picture book.* Warne, 1907

$8\frac{1}{8}″ \times 6\frac{1}{4}″$. 48 pp. including decorated t.p., half-title vignette, pictorial advert, hand-lettered dedication and 36 line drawings + inset front. and 7 plates in 3-colour half-tone letterpress.

Binding: Quarter cloth, green paper boards with oval half-tone on front ($3\frac{3}{4}″$ high).

36   *The House in the Wood and Other Old Fairy Stories*. Warne, [1909]

$9\frac{1}{4}″ \times 6\frac{5}{8}″$. 96 pp. including decorated half-title, pictorial advert and 46 line drawings in text + inset decorated t.p. and 7 plates in 3-colour half-tone letterpress.

Binding: Quarter cloth, cream paper boards with elaborate colour decoration on front by LLB.

The stories included are: 'The House in the Wood'; 'The Brave Little Tailor'; 'The Goblin and the Grocer'; 'The Bremen Town Musicians'; 'The Table, the Ass and the Cudgel'; 'The Jew in the Bramble Bush' (altered to 'The Old Man in the Bramble Bush' in 1944, following complaints); 'The Vagabond'; 'Red Jacket, or the nose-tree'; 'The Straw, the Coal and the Bean'; and 'Snow-white and Rose-red'.

37   GEORGE F. HILL. *The Truth about Old King Cole and Other Very Natural Histories*. Warne, [1910]
$8\frac{5}{8}'' \times 6\frac{7}{8}''$. 64 pp. including decorative half-title, pictorial advert and 33 line drawings in text + inset front., decorated t.p. and 5 plates in 3-colour half-tone letterpress. Decorated end-papers, line.
Binding: Quarter cloth, brown paper boards with half-tone roundel on front ($4\frac{3}{4}''$ diam.).

38   *The Tailor and the Crow; an old rhyme with new drawings*. Warne, 1911
$7\frac{1}{2}'' \times 6\frac{1}{8}''$. 40 pp. with decorated t.p., half-title drawing, decorated dedication and 31 drawings in text + inset front. and 5 plates in 3-colour half-tone letterpress. Decorated end-papers, line.
Binding: Canvas boards, decorated front. with oblong half-tone illustration ($3\frac{1}{8}'' \times 3''$).

39   *The Man in the Moon; a nursery rhyme picture book* [cover title]. Warne, [1913]
$10'' \times 8''$. 12 pp. with 12 line drawings in text + 8 plates in 3-colour half-tone letterpress.
Binding: Limp linen wrap-round with colour designs on outer face and line drawings on inner faces by LLB.

40   *Oranges and Lemons; a nursery rhyme picture book* [cover title]. Warne, [1913]
As previous item.
These two titles were issued as the first series of the 'Nursery Rhyme Picture Books' in one volume in 1913. Bound in cream paper boards with cloth spine and colour picture on front by LLB. See also following entries.

41   *Little Bo-peep; a nursery rhyme picture book* [cover title]. Warne, [1922]
As above.
Binding: Grey/green paper wrap-round designed as above.

42   *This Little Pig Went to Market; a nursery rhyme picture book* [cover title]. Warne, [1922]
As previous item.
These two titles formed the second series of one-volume 'Nursery Rhyme Picture Books', which was issued in 1922 along with a one-volume collection of the four titles in both series: *Ring O'Roses*, bound in blue cloth boards. All eight titles in the 'Nursery Rhyme' and 'Children's Books' series were later issued in smaller size as 'Leslie Brooke's Little Books' ($7'' \times 5\frac{1}{2}''$) bound in coloured paper boards.

43   LAWRENCE P. JACKS. *Mad Shepherds and Other Human Studies*. Williams & Norgate, 1923

$8\frac{5}{8}'' \times 5\frac{1}{2}''$. 260 pp. Inset front. and 5 plates tipped on heavy grey paper, line.

    A previous edition, with a frontispiece only by LLB, was published in 1910

44   ROBERT H. CHARLES. *A Roundabout Turn.* Warne, 1930

$7\frac{3}{4}'' \times 6''$. 48 pp. including decorated t.p. and 25 line drawings in text + inset front. and 3 plates in 3-colour half-tone letterpress. Decorated end-papers with frog roundel by LLB stamped in brown.

Binding: Orange cloth.

45   L. LESLIE BROOKE. *Johnny Crow's New Garden.* Warne, 1935

$8\frac{1}{4}'' \times 6''$. 48 pp. including decorated t.p. and dedication drawing and 37 other line drawings + inset front. and 7 plates in 3-colour half-tone letterpress. Decorated end-papers in line.

Binding: Quarter cloth, blue paper boards with oblong colour half-tone on front ($4'' \times 3''$). This is repeated on the blue dust-wrapper.

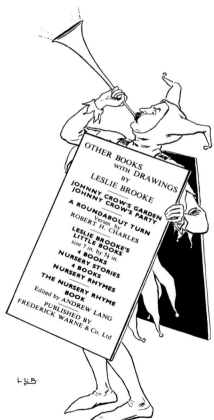

Index

Index